BIG

SE

XY

BARTOLO COLÓN
IN HIS OWN WORDS

with Michael Stahl
Illustrations by Meagan Ross

Abrams Image, New York

For Adriana

Prologue

I'm sitting on the roof of my Hummer, my legs dangling through the skylight into the back seat. The car is slowly winding downhill on the main road of the place where I grew up: El Copey, part of Altamira, a town in the northernmost province of the Dominican Republic. Lining the sidewalks on either side of me are the short, colorful buildings I've seen here since I was a little boy. Straight ahead of me in the distance is one of the area's many, many large mountains.

They say that when Christopher Columbus showed up, he saw the landscape and said, "Look at the heights!" That's about what "Altamira" translates to in English.

I am not alone on this road. I'm completely surrounded by people. I can't count how many. It seems like everyone from Altamira—and plenty more from other places, north and south, like Puerto Plata and Navarrete—is out here celebrating with me.

I was just named the Cy Young Award winner as the best pitcher in the American League for the 2005 season. As the car moves forward, people jump up to shake my hand and give me high fives. I know and love many of them. The rest know me and love me, too, I guess.

The reason they love me today is that I bought cases and cases of beer and put each bottle up for sale at just one Dominican peso, or about thirty-three American cents. In my hands is a bottle of rum. Soon it will be replaced by a sparkling cider.

At the outdoor community recreation area where the parade started, there's a big sound system that I had set up blasting music, and there's tons of food—mounds of rice and beans and roasted chicken and pork, everything. Riding below me is my wife, and in a few cars behind me are my parents, my brother and five sisters, and my three sons. My fourth will arrive in three years.

This parade is only about the midway point of the celebration. Three days ago, I was at the nearby field I had built, which would become the center of the Bartolo Colón Baseball Academy, where teenage boys train to

They say that when Christopher Columbus showed up, he saw the landscape and said, "Look at the heights!" That's about what "Altamira" translates to in English.

BARTOLO COLÓN

become Major League Baseball players like me. A representative of mine in the United States called me while I was at the field. He said I needed to be ready for a phone call from Major League Baseball's main office. Many of my best friends were with me, and there was a lot of noise, so I locked myself into a car, where it was quiet. They all followed me and stood around the car. The phone rang, and the voice on the other line said, "Mr. Colón, congratulations, you've won the Cy Young Award." I was overcome with emotion, and I could not speak. My friends were tapping on the window, saying, "Bartolo, what is it? What did they say?" The only thing I could do was smile and give them a thumbs-up. When I did that, they screamed. They knew what it meant.

That was when the party began. Word spread through the town, and people started coming together.

I went to the farm where my mother and father live to tell them the news. Of course, my mom and dad were

always very supportive of me, and they cried from the excitement.

I was again speechless. My father told me to jump up and down three times to snap myself out of it. I always listen to my father—well, almost always—so that's what I did, and it worked. Later, when I received the Cy Young Award plaque, I gave it to him and my mother.

After talking to them, I went for a stroll to my friend Mino's house. I needed a quiet place again, for another phone call—a conference call with reporters from the US. When that was over, I finally went into town for some fun.

In the days leading up to my trip down the three-kilometer parade route through Altamira, the party continued, as it did for a few days afterward. In the years since—while I continued my career and after I threw my last pitch in the Majors on September 22, 2018—there would be many more parties, in Altamira and elsewhere, celebrating me and my career.

My life hasn't always been one big party, though. Before I became a professional ballplayer, there were a lot of hardships, no different than those of many people in the Dominican Republic and around the world. And during my time as a pitcher, I experienced many struggles and tragedies—some no different than those of others, some very unique and at times impossible to comprehend.

But it all began, fittingly, in a land of steep valleys and incredible peaks.

BARTOLO COLÓN

I was born on May 24, 1973, the third child to Miguel Valerio Colón and Adriana Morales De Colón. I have two older sisters, a younger brother, and two younger sisters. My five siblings and I lived in a three-room house in the hills of El Copey. Our home was about the size of a two-car garage, give or take, with a living room and two bedrooms. At night we slept two to a bed, each with the other's feet next to their head. We were all very close and got along well.

BARTOLO COLÓN

The kitchen and the bathroom were outside, behind the house. For entertainment, we had a black-and-white TV, but most of the time we were outdoors. For fun—and for food—I would throw rocks at fruits on trees to get them to fall to the ground. I did this very often with coconuts, though sometimes they wouldn't fall. When that happened, I would climb the tree and pull one off the branch.

My family and I never felt like we needed anything more than what we had. There was always food on the table, even though there was not a lot of money to spend. Every year for Christmas, Mom and Dad bought each of us one outfit—a pair of tennis shoes, pants, and a shirt—to wear on Sundays. The rest of the days I wore sandals, shorts, and T-shirts, mostly, which were bought whenever there was an opportunity.

What is there to say about my parents? Both my father and mother were very good to me. They raised their children to believe in God, to give thanks to Him for both the good things and the bad things that happen in life. My mom and I had a very special bond. She took great care of all her children, but for me, she was always the person I could joke around with. We laughed together and had

14

For fun—and for food—I would throw rocks at fruits on trees to get them to fall to the ground. I did this very often with coconuts, though sometimes they wouldn't fall. When that happened, I would climb the tree and pull one off the branch.

15

BARTOLO COLÓN

some good times. My father is a little more serious and old-fashioned, but he's also very smart and kind in his own way. He's an excellent person, and everyone in the town loved him when I was a boy. He always wanted the best things for me, and from him I learned everything, especially how to work.

Next to the house was my father's grocery store, where he sold rice, beans, sugar, all the items you'd expect. But his specialties were avocado, coffee, and cacao, because behind our house he had a field with trees that grew them.

By the time I was about eight or nine years old, I was helping him pick avocado, coffee beans, and cacao off the trees in his field. I worked with him almost every single day. During the week, I would go to school from 8:00 a.m. until noon. I wasn't much of a student, to be honest; I liked helping my father. Not only did I pick fruit from the trees, I also used this machine he had that took the pulp casings off the coffee beans. To make it work, you put the coffee fruit into a pit and turned a lever around and around and around, over and over and over again. The coffee beans with their fruit stripped off would fall out of the bottom into a sack. I had to carry many heavy sacks of coffee beans and other fruits and vegetables from the field, up hills and down hills, to my house and to my dad's store.

To help me with my many chores, when I was about thirteen or fourteen years old, my father bought me a special gift, one that I treasure to this day, even though he is no longer with us: my very own pet donkey, Pancho.

Pancho was a good donkey. Pancho meant so much to me because it was my father who gave him to me. I would strap heavy sacks of fruit and coffee beans on Pancho's back and walk him from the fields to the store and my house. One time I loaded him up with twenty bags of coffee, which weighed two hundred pounds. When I would pull down avocados, I would load him up with two hundred of them. Sometimes I would ride on Pancho's back, but even then, that was for work, when Pancho had to drag a heavy load.

One day, around five years after my father gave him to me, Pancho was walking along a four-lane road and saw a female donkey on the other side of it. Pancho ran after her, hard—and when I say "hard," I don't mean "fast." As he chased after the female donkey, a car slammed into Pancho and killed him.

When that happened, I cried a lot.

BARTOLO COLÓN

A few years after I started working for my dad in the fields was when I began to play baseball. My father didn't teach me the game, though I used to watch him play softball sometimes. I mostly learned from my friends. There was one small field pretty close to where I lived, but we could make a baseball diamond out of any open area. Tin cans would be used as bases, or sometimes we'd put down milk cartons.

A lot of the time we didn't have gloves, so we'd throw the baseballs at the can or carton bases to record outs. We learned how to throw accurately that way. If you can hit a soup can with a baseball, you should be able to hit a grown man's chest. We'd tape up the baseballs when they got damaged, and when we didn't have one, we'd stuff socks to make one. When we didn't have a bat, we would just use an orange tree branch or some other piece of wood.

Early on I mostly played catcher, but when I was about thirteen or fourteen years old I pitched my first game at Rancho Nuevo, a much bigger field. To get there I would walk through the hills of Altamira for almost an hour. My parents were never worried about me. Some of the time when I was playing they didn't know it, because I snuck away from my father to get out of work, which made him mad when he found out.

He got very mad at me another time, when I stole a pack of cigarettes from his store. When I was a kid I was very quiet and did not get into trouble. But someone had told me that if you bring one of the managers of a baseball team a pack of cigarettes, he'll put you in the game. So I took the pack of cigarettes and gave it to the manager, but he didn't let me play. The team they were up against was too strong that day. I cried when I couldn't play. Then my mom and dad found out I stole the cigarettes, and they hit me with a belt on my butt. I cried again. That was a bad day for me.

Later on, once my father saw how much I loved baseball, he let me play a lot more. But even if my parents knew I was at the field, so far away from our home, my grandparents lived close by, and it seemed like everybody knew everybody in the area. It was safe—a lot safer than it is today.

We played two games, a doubleheader, all the time. The team who invited the others to come and play would bring food for everybody. One day I played catcher during the morning game. For the afternoon game, my team had no pitcher.

I volunteered.

I won that game, and after that I was always the pitcher. I liked pitching because as a pitcher you are always in control of the game, like the conductor of an orchestra.

BARTOLO COLÓN

HEY, ALBERT DIAZ, WHAT'S YOUR BEST BIG SEXY STORY?

The celebration Bartolo received when he won the Cy Young Award in 2005—that was the greatest event that has ever occurred in the history of Altamira. It was the biggest party with one of the most famous merengue groups of all time, Los Hermanos Rosario. There was the controversy, too, that the beer was only one peso. That's something that nobody is ever going to see again. It was unforgettable for me.

Bartolo has always shown solidarity with the community. He bought El Copey a fire truck; he built the baseball academy; he builds houses for people in the area who need them. He's never said no to someone; he's always giving, and to me that's why he is where he is today.

—ALBERT DIAZ
Trainer at the Bartolo Colón
Baseball Academy

I learned early on that when you pitch in the Dominican, the bigger the city, the better the competition—and the better you get. That was the advice that was given to me and my father by some local scouts: Always try to progress by pitching in the next biggest city.

After throwing at Rancho Nuevo all those years, I started playing on teams that would get invited to other places, like La Sierra and La Lomota, driving a half hour to an hour to get there. Then I pitched in Dominican League games in cities like Navarrete, Puerto Plata, and Santiago, growing stronger with each step, as each city grew, too.

Local scouts started to notice me when I was about seventeen. Between all that work in the fields and turning the lever to pulp the coffee, my pitching arm was strong. The rest of my body was, too, especially my legs, from walking all those hills.

By then, I'd stopped going to school. I just worked and played baseball. On the first day of seventh grade, my father took me to the school. We had to walk three or four kilometers.

We stood in front of the school, and he said, "Well, son, what do you think?"

I said, "Dad, I don't know."

"Do you want to study, or do you want the *collín*?" A *collín* is like a machete, so my father was asking if I wanted to work.

I said I wanted the *collín*. He bought me one, and in addition to working with him in his field, I went to work for the government. From 8:00 a.m. until 4:00 p.m., five days a week, I climbed trees along the road and cut down the overgrown branches.

But even with those two jobs, I always made time for baseball.

26

At first, I would pitch bullpen sessions for scouts who were fellow Dominicans, guys who were in-country with connections to Major League teams up north, hunting for talent. With them, I was never anxious; it was like pitching in front of an old friend or family member. But I felt endless nervousness when I met Minnie Mendoza and Johnny Gordo, who are Americans. They were in the Dominican representing the Cleveland Indians. To us players down there, they're the big bosses—the ones who recommend players for contracts. The Kansas City Royals and Los Angeles Dodgers were the only other teams who scouted me.

Minnie and Johnny had me pitch one day in Santiago in a bullpen. I threw twenty pitches, and even though I was nervous, I threw eighteen strikes. But the hardest I threw was only eighty-four miles per hour. Still, they liked me, and three days later, they saw me in game action. The hardest I threw that day was eighty-six miles per hour. I heard that some people with the Indians didn't want to sign me because they didn't think I threw hard enough. But Minnie and Johnny told them, "Sign him because he's a baseball player."

That became official about one month after my twentieth birthday. Of course, I was very happy to be a professional pitcher, and one for a Major League organization like the Indians. My father was very proud of me, but he was always telling me how proud he was, as a father to me and my brother and sisters as well. So a contract with a big league team wasn't treated like some huge accomplishment, really.

BARTOLO COLÓN

I got a $3,000 signing bonus, which back then was a lot of money in my mind. Five hundred dollars went to the two scouts who helped get me signed: Virgilio Perez Veras and Winston Llenas. They told the Indians about me first. I kept just $400 for myself and gave the rest of the money to my father, who very smartly bought a lot of land that is now worth much more.

28

But once you sign your contract, it's only the beginning. To me, playing in the Dominican Republic's cities, in their league games, I already felt as though I'd made the Majors. But, like a baby learning to walk, once I signed with the Indians, I was only just starting to see how challenging it is to be a professional with a Major League organization, or even to make a Major League roster.

In my mind, though, all I needed to do was respect my elders—a lesson I learned from my parents. In baseball, that translates to "listen to the coaches." You have to work hard and stay disciplined, sure, but the only way you can get better on the field is to take advice from people who have been around the game a long time. I thank God that it worked for me.

I heard that some people with the Indians didn't want to sign me because they didn't think I threw hard enough. But Minnie and Johnny told them, "Sign him because he's a baseball player."

BARTOLO COLÓN

HEY, JOSÉ ANTONIO TORRES REYES, WHAT'S YOUR BEST BIG SEXY STORY?

I met Bartolo in 1999, but when he was a schoolboy, my mother was one of his teachers. She would take attendance and say, "Where's Bartolo?" The other students would say, "He's out back." My mother went to look for him and found him behind the school, throwing rocks at fruit—mangoes, oranges; he would even throw them at coconuts.

She told him, "You aren't going to be a good student; you're going to be a good baseball player," because she saw his strong arm and his good throwing form.

My mother did tell me he was a genius at math, though.

—JOSÉ ANTONIO TORRES REYES
General manager at the Bartolo Colón Baseball Academy

I was signed for the 1994 season, so in 1993, I pitched in the Dominican Summer League for my country's beloved Águilas Cibaeñas, in Santiago. They're like the New York Yankees down there. My father was a huge fan of theirs when I was a boy—so I was, too, of course. It was a tremendous honor to pitch for the Águilas, but before I knew it, I was headed to the United States for the first time.

I was a large mixed bag of emotions. I felt very happy because I was going to leave the Dominican Republic and live the dream of playing in America—a dream I shared with many other Dominican boys. With God's help I wanted to see to it that my family lived a better life. But I cried a lot the night before I traveled to the US, and after I arrived in Winter Haven, Florida, for Minor League training camp, I cried every day for two weeks straight. I had never been away from my family. It's not that I felt completely alone, because I had friends—my new teammates—but still I felt sad. I thought about leaving baseball and returning to the Dominican Republic to be with my parents. I missed them so much, and it was a challenge just to talk to them. It was not like it is today, with cell phone technology—and the fact that I can afford cell phones for my family. My parents and I would have to plan our phone calls. They would be at a friend's or relative's house in places like Navarrete, a forty-minute drive away from where they lived. I'd tell my dad or my mom at the end of the phone call, "I'll call you next week at this same time, at this same number."

But after I was in Winter Haven for a couple of weeks, my father told me, "Son, you have to make an effort." I always tried to absorb his words, so all I could reply was, "Dad, I'm going to get you out from the bottom." That's how my time in the US started, and my father supported me very much. I sucked up all that sadness until I got what I wanted. I began working hard.

I also had support from my wife, Rosanna, who I married in 1995. We'd met a few years earlier, when her brother, Fermín Vargas, began dating my sister Miguela. They didn't last like me and Rosanna did, though.

I had trouble talking to Rosanna, like I had trouble talking to everyone else, because I was so shy—and she was so beautiful. But Rosanna was shy and quiet, too, like me, and for some reason my mother was always trying to get us together, inviting her over to our house.

When I would go to see Rosanna, her parents wouldn't let us leave the front porch of their house for a long time. I could only see her from 6:00 p.m. until 9:00 p.m., not a minute earlier or later. So we just talked as much as we could on the porch. After a while her parents finally let me take her for a walk into town for an ice cream. Her mother told me, "Come get her at two p.m., and she has to be back here at six p.m."

When I went to her parents' house to ask for her hand in marriage, I asked my father to come with me, but he refused. He thought it was a silly game between me and Rosanna, that we weren't serious because we were so young. But that was one of the rare times in his life he was wrong.

I went to Rosanna's parents' house alone, and when I started to talk to Rosanna's father, Fermín Sr., I couldn't get the words out. I was so nervous. I said, "Fermín, I'm in love with your . . . ," and my mouth would not say "daughter."

My future brother-in-law, Fermín Jr., finished my proposal for me.

35

After Indians spring training, I was off to live full-time in my first American city: Burlington, North Carolina.

I shared an apartment there with two other players from the organization's rookie-ball team, the Burlington Indians of the Appalachian League. It was me, Julio Perez, and Rafael Mesa—the brother of former Major League closer José Mesa.

The rent was around $600 a month. Even though I was only being paid around $200 every two weeks, I still made sure I sent my dad some money: $15, $20, or $30. My roommates and I didn't do much. Between the little money we had and the lot of time we spent practicing and playing baseball, there wasn't much we *could* do. Sometimes we had to walk forty-five minutes to get to the stadium. Minnie Mendoza was in Burlington with me, though, working as the team's hitting coach, and sometimes he would drive me to the stadium and back. He helped me adjust to the changes quite a bit.

Road trips were all by bus, sometimes five- or six-hour drives, to places like Bluefield, Virginia, and Princeton, West Virginia. The travel was tough, but it also brought me and my teammates closer together, especially the other players from the Dominican Republic. I struggled to learn English, but only because—like most people from the Dominican countryside—I kept to myself. From my perspective, the difference between Dominicans from the country and Dominicans from the city is that those from the country are always working, from the time they're very young. The families are humble and quiet, and that becomes your norm as a child. The Dominicans who live in cities seem to have more freedom to spend time with their friends. Many of them work, too, but I guess because there are more people living close to them, it's easier for them to socialize more often. They tend to be more open and talkative, in my opinion.

In spite of all that personal hardship, though, I felt good pitching while I was with the Burlington Indians. That year I finished 7–4, with a 3.14 ERA. When I'd arrived, I was throwing about eighty-eight miles per hour. By the end of the season, my velocity was up to ninety-six miles per hour. I honestly don't know how that increase was possible. I was exercising a lot, doing countless wind sprints, if you can believe it. I always ran very fast, and that helped build up my leg strength even more. All the while, as I threw, my arm got stronger, too, but as I always say, it really was just a blessing from God.

Another thing that might have helped me is the good food in America. When you come from the Dominican, you don't know what a diet is. The way I ate in the Dominican was the way I ate in the States. I didn't know what protein was, or carbs or whatever. I didn't know anything. Just to eat.

Once Minor League spring training camp broke, we had to buy our own food, but before the season started, at the stadium there would be, like, a buffet set up. The Indians would give us an $8 daily stipend for lunch and dinner. We could take what we wanted, but if it cost more than $8, we would pay for it out of pocket.

I ate more pork than anything else. I would get the steaks a lot, too, but to me, the way it was cooked, it was like raw. I'd always send it back to the kitchen so they'd cook it well-done. I ate some vegetables—mostly mashed potatoes, things like that.

BARTOLO COLÓN

Breakfast was a juice and a sandwich and that's it. There were a lot of bagels.

During the season, while living with my roommates, I did most of the cooking. Rafael Mesa cooked sometimes, too, and we made what we would always make in the Dominican: chicken and pork, rice and beans, all that good stuff.

I was beginning the Big Sexy metamorphosis, I guess, putting on weight, which also helped me build up my velocity.

At the end of the Appalachian League's three-month season in 1994, I went back to the Dominican Republic. I hadn't even thought I was going to go back to the DR—for all I knew I'd just stay in America during the off-season—but thank God I did. Throughout the winter I picked coffee, cacao, and avocado with my dad in his field, just like I had when I was a kid. It was very soothing to be close to him again, not to mention my mother.

I wasn't certain that the Indians would bring me back to the States for the next season, though I did feel as if I'd played well enough to earn an invitation.

Winston Llenas—who's from Santiago and played in the Major Leagues for the California Angels—oversaw the Cleveland Indians' operations in the Dominican. He

40

was the man who gave the order to sign me, after Johnny Gordo and Minnie Mendoza told him about me. Winston, who everyone calls "Chilote," held on to the passports of all the Dominican players during the off-season. He'd take them from us as we left the plane in the DR. The Indians did this to keep players who they did not invite back to play in the US from reentering the country. It would make the Indians look bad if their former players were going to the US without a real job waiting for them—and with their passports, they could get in legally. If they stayed after their work visa expired, then they'd be in the country *illegally*. The players the Indians released got their passports returned to them once their work visa expired.

I didn't see anything wrong with any of that; I just wasn't sure when I'd see my passport again. But one day Chilote told me, "You're going to travel again," and I got very happy. In the spring of 1995, I was back in Florida at Minor League camp for the Indians, competing hard. But shortly before camp broke, they said I was returning to rookie-ball in Burlington, and once again I was upset. I was so disappointed the Indians didn't promote me that I thought about quitting and going home again. This time it was Minnie Mendoza who encouraged me to stay, so I did.

Good fortune was on the way for me, though. Unfortunately, it was at the expense of someone else. I don't recall the gentleman's name, but a pitcher who was set to pitch for the Kinston Indians—the next level up, in the

A-ball Carolina League—broke his arm. In fact, I'd been throwing in a bullpen session right next to him just a few minutes before he was injured. Kinston needed a pitcher, and I went seven scoreless innings. I stayed there for the rest of the season.

In Kinston, North Carolina, I roomed with Enrique Wilson, who would go on to make the Majors and play alongside me with the Indians and, later, for a few other teams. César Ramos and Maximo De La Rosa, two pitchers, lived in the apartment as well. The three of them, as well as Rafael Mesa, were among the guys I stayed close with as we moved through the Minor Leagues together. I did become friends with other players who were not Latino, by the way. Bruce Aven, an outfielder who played briefly in the Majors for the Indians a couple of times, was very good to me. He helped me out a lot as I learned to live in a new country.

I was earning slightly more money in Kinston, but not much. Also, even though I'd moved up a level, the travel became even more grueling, with eight-hour bus rides to visit other stadiums. Regardless, I felt loose in Kinston. That year I won thirteen games and lost only three. I ended up with an ERA of 1.96, and I finished second in the Carolina League in wins and ERA. Glendon Rusch, who later made the Majors, beat me out in both categories. I did have the most strikeouts, however.

I was successful that season because I had better control of my pitches, which at that time were the four-seam fastball, the curveball, and the changeup. I'd learned

I struggled to learn English, but only because—like most people from the Dominican countryside— I kept to myself.

43

BARTOLO COLÓN

a very helpful trick from my coaches: Between starts, practice your windup in the mirror. Remember what you look like and what your body feels like going through the motions, and repeat the windup as best you can in the games. I took that very seriously.

I also learned the importance of strike one. It doesn't matter what pitch you use, but get strike one on the first pitch. From there you can work however you want, moving around the strike zone and using different pitches. That's what every good pitcher does.

The one thing I disagreed with my coaches about was that some of them wanted me to change my mechanics a bit, starting my windup with my hands at or above my head instead of in front of my chest. Even though they thought that might help, especially with my velocity, I was never comfortable with it. My own mechanics worked best for me.

Though I played very well that season in '95, I didn't finish it. One of the tendons in my right elbow became tender. I lost velocity in my pitches, and my arm got swollen. The team sent me to Cleveland to get an MRI, and they wanted me to undergo surgery. I refused. Nobody was going to cut my arm open then. I went back to Kinston, and as I rehabbed my elbow, I watched my teammates take the Carolina League championship, which was a great thrill. I felt disappointed in myself because I wanted to help the team until the end. I cried during that time, a lot. About then there was also talk that the Indians were going to trade me to the Toronto Blue Jays for David

Cone, which caused me some unease as well. (Cone wound up with the Yankees eventually.)

After the '95 season, I went back to my home in Altamira. I just rested my arm, and after about two weeks, I was back to 100 percent. It was another gift from God. I was now touted as Cleveland's number one prospect. The organization awarded me Minor League Player of the Year, in fact, which truly was an honor. I was much more confident I'd be back in the States for Minor League camp the next year than I had been the season before. But I still returned to work in my father's fields through the rest of the off-season, once again.

That was the last time I worked for my dad.

In 1996, the Indians invited me to their Major League spring training camp. I told my father the news, and he said, "All right, son. That's good. You do what you need to do to be a pitcher, and leave this to us." It was my dad's decision to have me retire from the cacao-, avocado-, and coffee-picking business so I could focus on my second career as a full-time professional ballplayer.

I can't begin to explain how excited I was to be at my first Major League training camp. For me, seeing guys who played on big-league fields, like Albert Belle, for the first time in person was like a dream.

That was also the year I really got to know Manny Ramirez. Though he spent his teens living in New York City, he was born in Santo Domingo, the Dominican Republic's capital. I have many friends in baseball, but if I had to choose one as my best friend, it would be him. We're about the same age and get along great. We played together for the Indians, as well as the Boston Red Sox and the Águilas in the Dominican, and we still text and call each other all the time.

People in the media and fans sometimes say that he's a weird guy; when he does strange things, it's always "Manny being Manny." To me, he's a tremendous person, and he's still the same person I met over twenty years ago. He has his ways, yes, but once anybody gets to know him, they learn that he is a cool guy. He does like to please people a lot, which I don't think many recognize. One time, in Cleveland, I asked him to meet me for dinner, and he said, "Yes, I'll be right there," but he never showed up. I didn't take that behavior from Manny as rude, though. I just don't think he likes saying no to friends, or people in general, ever.

I was overjoyed to be with the Indians that spring, but I didn't last long in camp. Shortly before preseason games were about to start, they began cutting players. I was the first one to be sent down to continue training with the Minor Leaguers. I wasn't ready for the Majors yet. This time, however, I wasn't discouraged. When camp broke, I was now in Double-A, with the Canton-Akron Indians, and by the end of the season, I was with the Buffalo Bisons of the Triple-A American Association League. Today, Triple-A teams and even some Double-A teams travel by plane. But back then, in '96, my teammates and I were still on buses, and the longest trip I can recall was sixteen hours. We drove from Canton, Ohio, to Portland, Maine, to play the Sea Dogs, which was the Florida Marlins' Double-A affiliate. My favorite part of those bus trips was getting *off* the bus, so we could pee.

I continued to get bigger, stronger, and better, though the Bisons needed me out of the bullpen, which I wasn't used to and didn't like at that time, to be honest. I had a 0.00 ERA with that team, but a 1.74 ERA in Canton-Akron, where I pitched primarily as a starter.

But that was my last full season in the Minors.

HEY, BIG SEXY, WHO'S YOUR FAVORITE TEAMMATE?

Answer

Manny Ramirez,
of the Cleveland Indians and Boston Red Sox.

I made my Major League debut on April 4, 1997. I was twenty-three years old and pitching for the Cleveland Indians. Our opponent: the Anaheim Angels.

Throughout spring training, my second with the Indians' big leaguers, I was competing for a spot in the starting rotation. I had no idea whether I'd make the team, but by the end of the spring I'd been pitching pretty well, and it came down to me and Steve Karsay for the fifth starter slot. It wasn't looking good for me during my final spring start, though—the one that would decide if I'd stay up in the Majors or go down to the Minors. Pitching against the Atlanta Braves, early on I gave up a couple of walks and a home run to Chipper Jones, their future Hall of Fame third baseman. Then I came back and struck out six in a row. I went five innings overall but lost the game, so I thought I was going back to the Minors. However, Karsay gave up four home runs in his last spring start, and afterward the Indians' manager, Mike Hargrove, came up to me and said, "Congratulations. You made the team."

I was so excited. Back at my apartment, I cried tears of joy. I called my dad, and he was excited, too, of course, as well as my mom. Both were congratulating me and crying. It was very special.

They missed my first-ever start, however, because I didn't yet know the process of how I could get them to the United States—finding a visa and all that. Plus, the Indians had to travel to Oakland for our first two games of the season before traveling to Anaheim to face the Angels. Before I knew it, I was on the mound making my Major League debut.

This start was much like my previous one in spring training—except it actually counted. I gave up two runs in the first inning, and in the second, Gary DiSarcina hit the first home run I ever gave up, a two-run shot to left field. He'd only hit three more home runs the rest of the year.

When I got back to the dugout after that inning, a few teammates said, "Welcome to the Major Leagues."

I was very nervous at the start of that game. It was incredible to think I was pitching in the Major Leagues, it really was. But I settled down, went five innings, and got a no-decision. Albie Lopez came on in relief and pitched four scoreless innings, but we lost the game in the eleventh inning on a walk-off grand slam by Tim Salmon.

It was a tough start to the '97 season, one that set a tone for myself, personally—though the team turned out to be just fine. Once I got over the initial excitement of being in the Majors, reality set in a little bit. I don't fault the organization at all, because I did not pitch well in the Majors that season, but the Indians had me going up and down, between Triple-A and the Big Club, like a yo-yo. I switched teams I think six or seven times, which I'd later come to realize is relatively normal for a young player like I was then. But all the travel was especially difficult because Rosanna was pregnant with our first son that year, and I didn't want to cause her stress. I made $150,000, which was nice, but that meant nothing when it came to worrying about my wife and our boy during the many long drives between Cleveland and Buffalo. The constant movement also had to do with strategy and scheduling. Mike Hargrove wanted to use four starters as often as the team could, so anytime there was an off day in the schedule, or a rainout, they wouldn't need a fifth starter for that turn in the rotation. So I'd go back down to Triple-A and pitch for the Bisons.

In early May I was up with the Indians, in Detroit to play the Tigers. In my hotel room the night before my start, the phone rang. I picked up the receiver, and a man's voice on the other line said, "If you don't pitch a good game tomorrow, we are going to kill you and your wife and your family." They read my home address to me. I was so scared. I called a member of the Indians staff, and they called the police to investigate.

I barely slept that night, and starting the next morning, I thought about what might happen all day long before I took the mound. I was praying to God for protection on the bus ride to the stadium. Even though I was very worried about my family, I threw a good game, going six innings and giving up two runs. We did lose the game, and afterward, outside the ballpark, I was signing merchandise for some fans. Then three police officers took me back to the hotel in the back of their car and asked me what happened. Luis Isaac, the longtime Indians bullpen coach, was translating for me. Major League Baseball sent security to escort me out to dinner to protect me, too.

That night, my phone rang again, and the voice said that because I played well, they weren't going to hurt anyone. They also said that they'd follow up with me, and the next time they needed me to do well, they'd let me know. The team switched me from one hotel room to another, but then I got another call from the same person. The police were listening in and trying to trace it. They were not successful, but they started to think, because I'd switched rooms and the calls still came, that it might have been one of my teammates playing a prank.

If that was a joke, it wasn't funny. I didn't like that.

Back down in the Minors, the hitters are not as selective as those in the Majors; that's the big difference between the two levels, in my opinion. I finished with a 2.22 ERA in 10 starts with the Bisons, and threw a no-hitter at home in Buffalo.

That was one of the greatest games I've ever pitched. I walked the second batter of the game, who then got thrown out trying to steal second base. Nobody else got on base, so I only faced twenty-seven hitters, the fewest you can possibly see in a baseball game. It was a very emotional night for me. It was one of the first of a few times in my career when I was so nervous my knees were shaking. As I took to the mound for the ninth inning, I could hardly stand. The Bisons also won the league's championship that season.

What was even more amazing that year was my Cleveland teammates making the World Series. They upset the defending champions, the New York Yankees, in the American League Division Series, and then upset the Baltimore Orioles in the Championship Series as well. I was not on the postseason roster, but I watched the playoffs and the World Series at home, in the Dominican Republic, with my wife and newborn son, Bartolo Jr. Against the Florida Marlins, the Indians went all the way to Game 7, the eleventh inning, but could not win the championship. I felt horrible for my teammates, most of whom never played in a World Series game again.

57

BARTOLO COLÓN

HEY, BIG SEXY, WHO'S GOT YOUR FAVORITE UNIFORM?

Question

Answer

The Cleveland Indians

Going into the 1998 spring training camp, I was probably seventh on the Indians' depth chart for starting pitchers, seemingly destined to begin the season in Triple-A. But the two guys ahead of me got hurt. I pitched well that spring, made the team, and I remained in the big leagues for good. Though I didn't think this way at the time, I guess I was finally ready for that stage, and I pitched so well overall, thank God, that I didn't let the Indians think they could send me down, even when the other players were healthy.

I had a bad start against the Blue Jays in late May, where I gave up seven runs, but after that, heading into the All-Star break, I won six of seven starts with three complete games, including one shutout. I didn't allow more than three runs in any of those starts and lowered my ERA from a respectable 3.19 to 2.46, which led the league at that point.

Because the Indians had made the World Series in '97, Mike Hargrove was managing the American League All-Stars in '98, and he was kind enough to put me on the team.

In my first full season as a Major Leaguer, I was an All-Star. I still can't believe that. I was very honored. I was on a staff with guys like Roger Clemens and my old countryman Pedro Martínez. I was in the clubhouse with Cal Ripken Jr., Ken Griffey Jr., and Roberto Alomar. It was incredible.

I even got the win in that game, but that was luck. In the one inning I pitched, I gave up a triple to Devon White, then I walked Mark McGwire, and Barry Bonds hit a three-run home run to right field. This was at Coors Field in Colorado, and in that part of the stadium they had banners for each team hanging off the facade of the upper deck. Bonds hit the banner for his own team, the San Francisco Giants. I like that Bonds was able to do that, and as Joe Morgan said in the game's broadcast, I did Bonds a favor by throwing him back-to-back change-ups. That was an error on my part because my fastball was one hundred miles per hour most of that inning; my adrenaline level was so concentrated. In regular-season games, I was usually around ninety-six or ninety-seven back then.

Thankfully, the American League hitters got the lead back for us in the next inning, which the team held on to 'til the end.

After that, I had a few decent starts in the second half of the season, but I did not do as well as I had before the break. I was still learning so much and only beginning to understand how to get through a 162-game season, physically and mentally.

The last game I pitched for Cleveland in 1998, though, was my best, and certainly my most memorable of the year.

I'd started what happened to be the closeout game against the Red Sox, in Game 4 of the American League Division Series. Even though it was the first playoff game of my career, and it was at Fenway Park, I actually don't recall much about it. It was unbelievable to be pitching in the playoffs, on that stage, at such a young age, but my mind is mostly a blank when it comes to that game. Nomar Garciaparra hit a home run off me; I remember that. It was the only run I gave up, but I left the mound in the sixth inning on the losing side, down 1–0. My teammates picked me up, though, rallying late, and we finished off Boston.

But then in the American League Championship Series we had to face the Yankees—and not just *any* Yankees. That was the year they won 114 regular-season

63

HEY, IVELIS PEÑA, WHAT'S YOUR BEST BIG SEXY STORY?

Early in his career with the Indians, toward the beginning of the season, there was a game where Bartolo didn't last the first inning. They hit him hard. After the game, he says to me, "Ivelis, I'm not any good."

He was very frustrated, and I looked at him, and I said, "Bartolo, you have to know that words can really dictate your life. One bad game is just one bad game. You can't say that because you got to this point for a reason, because you were good; you just have to keep on trying."

I kind of scolded him for talking that way, and he was surprised because I think he thought I was going to encourage what he was saying. But after that, every time I would see him on a day he was going to pitch, I'd say, "Come on, Bartolo, no-hitter," or "OK, Mr. Cy Young, no-hitter." He would just look at me and listen, but he wouldn't respond. He was so shy.

We were being so positive with him and working on his mental approach—me, a security guard who worked in the family room, and his wife, Rosanna, who had perfect attendance at Jacobs Field. She came early, before the game, and stayed the whole game. She showed him unconditional support.

Well, Bartolo didn't quit. He became an All-Star and, later, the Cy Young Award winner.

—IVELIS PEÑA
Jacobs Field family room employee with the Cleveland Indians

In my first full season as a Major Leaguer, I was an All-Star. I still can't believe that. I was very honored.

games, the most by any team in Major League history at the time. They were loaded. They had great starting pitching, an amazing bullpen, and one of the toughest lineups you could imagine.

If you need a reminder of some of the players on that team, here are a few names: Derek Jeter, Mariano Rivera, Paul O'Neill, Andy Pettitte, Tino Martinez, David Cone, Chuck Knoblauch, Bernie Williams, Jorge Posada, Orlando "El Duque" Hernández, David Wells, and Scott Brosius. They had guys like Tim Raines coming off the bench, Chili Davis as their designated hitter, and they all were led by Joe Torre, who's now a Hall of Fame manager.

Before the series began, Mike Hargrove had a meeting with all the starting pitchers. He told me I was going to get the ball for the third game, and every night leading up to it I stayed up late watching video of the Yankees hitters. I hardly slept.

We were underdogs, and it was understandable why, but early in the series we stole a game at the old Yankee Stadium in New York: Game 2, a twelve-inning marathon famous for the Chuck Knoblauch play when he argued a call at first base on a throw from Tino Martinez. While the ball rolled behind him into the outfield during his protest, we scored the go-ahead run that won it for us.

When the Indians left New York, I got together with my father in Cleveland during the off day. I was about to start Game 3 at our home park, Jacobs Field, with a chance to give my team the series lead. I was going up against David Cone, who the Indians almost traded

BARTOLO COLÓN

me for that time. Cone won twenty games in '98, but my father told me, "Son, tomorrow's game is just like any other game you've pitched before. Don't feel pressured." I told him, "Yes, Dad, but it's the Yankees; it's not just any team." And he said, "No, no, you're going to have a good game. Go with God, son, and we'll talk after the game." I had it in my mind, then: I'd perform well, even under the circumstances.

The first three innings are like a dream to me, even now. My knees were shaking, I was so nervous. I wasn't really even thinking. But every pitcher desires to compete against the best lineups and against the best pitchers. That's what I always liked.

When it came to strategy, with that Yankees team there wasn't much to work with, so you just had to give it your all. I didn't have any big plans for them because at that time they didn't know me well, and I didn't know them. They only knew that I threw hard. Back then, against any team I always tried to strike out the first batter to make the rest of the inning maybe a little less difficult. Of course, the Yankees were so good I only finished with three strikeouts, and Knoblauch led the game off with a base hit. Then, with two outs Bernie Williams drove him in with another hit. Though they didn't score again, it really wasn't until after the third inning that I loosened up. From then on, I felt normal; the pressure I had on me went away.

I walked a few batters and gave up a couple of hits, but no more runs. I keep video of the ninth inning from that game on my phone and watch it every once in a while.

68

BIG SEXY

It's such a special memory. The crowd was so loud and intense, and when I struck out Tino Martinez to end the game, I couldn't hold back my excitement. I got chills seeing the fans so excited. I pumped my fist, and my teammates rushed the mound to congratulate me.

They told me so many good, encouraging things I think. I still didn't know English very well, much less than I do now, so I didn't understand what they were saying. I just smiled back at them. While we celebrated, as I walked off the field, I lost feeling in my legs again, I was so happy.

In the video you can see some nice Cleveland fans who made signs supporting the team and me. One of them even says "Pancho Power," but Pancho's name is misspelled, with an "o" in place of the "a." So instead it

BARTOLO COLÓN

reads "Poncho Power," which always makes me laugh. I never pitched while wearing a raincoat. I don't think the league would have allowed it. And I was good enough without one.

Outside the stadium, I saw my father, my mother, my wife, and my son, who was about a year old. I had tears rolling down my cheeks. My father told me how proud of me he was.

The Indians were confident we'd win the series at that point. We said to each other, "This is ours." Not only were we up two games to one, but we'd just beaten one of the Yankees' best pitchers, and we still had two more consecutive games at home, so that gave us a huge advantage. Plus, my teammates had beaten them in the playoffs the year before.

Unfortunately, we lost the next three games, and I didn't get the chance to pitch at Yankee Stadium in what would have been Game 7. Pitching there, in that historic stadium, in the biggest city in the United States—that really would have been exciting.

The Yankees went on to win the World Series that year, and the two after that—four in five seasons total. So I treasure that victory of mine in '98, when they were at their absolute best.

The only negative from that game was during an at bat against Joe Girardi. His bat broke apart and flew into the stands. I think a few people got hurt. I saw some blood, but I turned away quickly. I don't like to see things like that, but that night it did not break my concentration too much. I heard about a year later that some fans were suing Girardi and me. I think their lawyers sent a letter to me, but the Indians management intercepted it and sent it to the Players Association. I never saw the letter, and Major League Baseball handled the lawsuit. I don't think anything came of it because on the back of every ticket it says the league is not responsible for injuries from such incidents. Regardless, thankfully situations like that are more avoidable now with the longer protective screens down the stadium stands.

71

My time with the Cleveland Indians was incredible. I thank them so much for signing me, for the opportunity to play in the Major Leagues and to prove myself as a professional. Cleveland was where my wife and I first lived for a substantial amount of time in the United States and where our first son was raised. We led a fairly simple life, really. After games I would come home for dinner, prepared by my wife, and listen to music. I didn't go out to clubs or anything like that.

I was very focused on baseball. Today, when young players come up, I think a lot of them don't take the game very seriously. You see them joking around on the field. There wasn't nearly as much of that back when I started. I enjoyed playing, for sure, but I wanted to work hard, get better, and help my team. That was it.

I was not a saint, though. During my career with Cleveland, I started drinking a lot. When I was home with my wife, I'd only have a couple of drinks, but I was so afraid of flying that anytime I got on a plane I pretty much had to be drunk. That was a problem that stayed with me for years. I once even developed some trouble with my liver, it got that bad.

But in 1999 the Indians blessed me with a contract extension: $9 million for four years. With that money I eventually bought a home for my parents in Santiago and homes for some of my siblings. But after taxes and agent and lawyer fees, it's really not as much money as you think, and I wanted to do even more for them. Still, my family was more comfortable financially than ever before, which I was grateful for.

Many people helped me out in Cleveland. Charles Nagy did a lot for me, and then a Dodgers veteran named Orel Hershiser came over. He took me aside and began talking frequently with me and Jaret Wright as well. That's how you begin learning, and I thank God for all the support he gave me. I'd listen to him talk about how to approach batters and tried to do what he did. He'd show me different pitching grips, too, and how to not only pitch to an individual hitter but to strategize against an entire lineup. There are guys you just don't want to let beat you and your team, so maybe you sacrifice a walk and just concentrate on the batters who come after him—whatever you need to do to win the game.

I also learned the value of pitching inside and how to do it. Early in my career, I was always afraid of hitting batters with the ball. I sometimes saw that a batter was pretty strong, and I would say to myself, "If I hit one of them and he comes at me, what am I going to do then?"

One off-season, when I went back to the Dominican, Virgilio Perez Veras—one of the scouts who helped me get signed by the Indians—made me a dummy, and we'd stand it up next to home plate at a field. I could throw as hard as I wanted inside. At first I hit the dummy a lot, but eventually I learned where I could go effectively inside without hitting it.

After signing the contract extension, I began to gain more weight. In that famous photo of me right after I signed with the Indians at twenty years old—the one everyone says I look so skinny in—I was already 205 pounds. By the end of '98, I'd put on I think twenty pounds, but at one point I blew up to about 240 or 250. I was eating a lot of Chinese food, like chicken fried rice. And I loved Taco Bell and McDonald's, too.

I was throwing harder at that weight, but Cleveland actually offered me a bonus of $12,500 if I stayed at or under 225 pounds for a season. I tried to lose weight, but

I couldn't—at least not anything significant, and when I did, I noticed I'd lose velocity in my pitches.

In spring training one year, the Indians trainer Fernando Montes ordered me and Cecil Fielder—another famously big guy and a great home run hitter—to ride a two-person bicycle around the outside of the facility. He wanted us both to lose weight, and there was a catch: We couldn't sit down on the bike because there were no seats. We had to bike about a mile and a half like that, together, which meant we went around the complex three or four times.

I told Luis Isaac, the longtime bullpen coach for the Indians, that I was going to keep my weight, and if I gained weight, even better still because it made me a better pitcher.

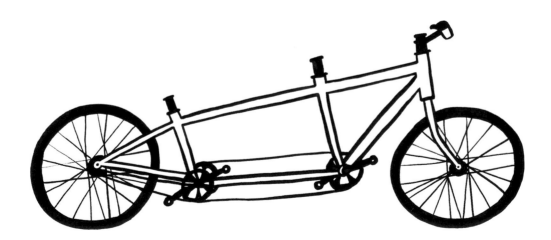

Montes also had me do a lot of running and some weight training, too. But I didn't lift heavy weights with my arms; that's not good for pitchers. My legs did the heavy lifting instead. I'd sometimes press over eight hundred pounds with my legs.

And when you work out as much as I did—and do—you pack on muscle. And muscle weighs more than fat. I think the uniform makes me look heavier than I really am; plus, as they say, when you're on TV, the camera adds ten pounds. When people see me in person, they always say that I'm nowhere near as big, or as fat, as they thought I would be.

HEY, OMAR VIZQUEL, WHAT'S YOUR BEST BIG SEXY STORY?

One of the funniest stories I can share with you is when his kids started going to school, obviously they were going to an American school, and they were getting good at speaking English.

I was talking to Bartolo one time, and I said, "How are your kids doing?"

He said, "Oh, they're doing great; you know, they're in school, and they're doing really well."

"That's great, I'm happy for you!" I said.

And he said, "Well, the only problem is now they speak all English, and I speak all Spanish, so I can't even talk to my own kids."

When I first met Bartolo I had already been with the Indians for a few years when he came to the team. He was really shy because he comes from a little town where there weren't too many people. I think he felt a little overwhelmed having so many people around him all the time. He also didn't speak English very much, so he was very introverted, very private; he was a guy who didn't share much. But he had a rifle arm; instead, I'll call it a cannon. He could throw ninety-five-plus for a hundred pitches and he never got tired. He was one of those guys who, when he took the mound, he went all out. Every team needs a guy like that, someone who can come back maybe on three days' rest and still throw ninety-five. He didn't think about pitch count; all he wanted to do was throw the ball.

But you always want to be connected to your teammates; it doesn't matter what language they speak. I noticed that he was a little introverted, and I wanted to get him involved in everything that we did with the team. Some of the ways to do that is you throw kids' birthday parties. Our kids were about the same age, so we wanted to get everyone together. When the team does baseball clinics for local kids, I'd make sure we brought him. It was very hard to get him involved because he was so reserved, but we were a little successful.

It was great to see how, at the end of his career, he was doing stuff that made everybody else laugh, like every time he'd go up to hit, he'd laugh with his teammates as he'd go back to the dugout. I don't think he would have dared to do anything like that with the Indians. You didn't see that from him; I think he would have been embarrassed. It was nice to see him come out of his shell. Obviously, in New York, being exposed to a lot of Latinos in and around the ballpark helped him a lot.

—OMAR VIZQUEL
Cleveland Indians teammate

In 2002, I began another year with the Indians. But I wouldn't finish it with the team. A little less than halfway through the season, I was looking good, with ten wins and a 2.55 ERA. But the team's record only had thirty-five wins next to thirty-nine losses. Cleveland still had a year and a half of control over me, and I didn't think they'd trade me.

Mark Shapiro, who's now the president and CEO of the Toronto Blue Jays, was the Indians general manager back then, and he even said to me during a road trip to Miami about that time, "You aren't leaving this team. Not even when you're dead."

Five days later he traded me to the Montreal Expos.

But by then I had a feeling it was coming. Twenty-four hours earlier, he asked me for my phone number—something he'd never done before. I'd also heard a few teams were offering Cleveland deals for me. I pitched my last game for the Indians, ironically, against the Expos in Montreal, where I slightly strained my oblique while batting. Two days later, the Indians were in Boston for a series against the Red Sox. The team sent me back to Cleveland for an MRI on my oblique, which came back negative, and Shapiro called me into his office at about 5:00 p.m. on June 27.

He started saying something to me like, "Hey, I want to explain something to you."

I just said, "Tell me where I'm going."

He kept talking to me but didn't answer my question, so I said, "I just want to know where I'm going. Don't give me explanations. Where am I going?"

"You're going to Montreal," he said. And the only thing I did was shake his hand and say, "Thank you very much. May God bless you," and I left.

He said to me again, "But let me explain to you."

"Don't explain anything to me," I said, stopping him. "You already traded me. What are you going to explain to me?"

BARTOLO COLÓN

83

That was it.

I was upset, but that was when I learned that baseball is a business. After the players they traded me for—Brandon Phillips, Cliff Lee, and Grady Sizemore—became All-Stars, I felt very happy about that.

They called it the Trade of the Decade, and some even said it was the Trade of the Century. I don't know if it was or wasn't, but I quickly felt very comfortable with the Expos. In the beginning it was like your first day at a new school, full of nerves. But the team had many Latin-born players, and they were like a family, welcoming me right into it. There was Andrés Galarraga, Tony Armas Jr., and Endy Chávez, from Venezuela; José Vidro, Javier Vázquez, and Wil Cordero, from Puerto Rico; Orlando Cabrera, from Colombia; and Fernando Tatís and Vladimir Guerrero from the Dominican Republic. Even Bruce Chen, whose grandparents migrated from China, hails from Panama.

Everybody on that team got along great, sincerely, and not just the Latino players. Thankfully, in part because I was so comfortable in Montreal, I was able to keep the rhythm I had with Cleveland going, and I finished the year strong.

I was supposed to have all this pressure on me because Montreal was trying their best to make the playoffs. For years they had had trouble drawing fans, and many speculated that a playoff run would help keep the team in the city. I was the guy who'd help make that happen. None of those things worked out, unfortunately. It was one of the best pitching stretches of my career, but I was just focused on baseball, like always. The fans really embraced me and were pretty loud during some of my games; however, I couldn't worry about whether the team could stay where it was.

Plus, I was in the National League, where there's no designated hitter batting in place of the pitcher like in the American League. I had to work on my hitting.

I wasn't nervous about that, though. I was looking forward to it. Growing up, playing catcher, I hit all the time, and I was pretty good, too. With Montreal I'd take a lot of batting practice. Still, the results weren't very good. The decade-long layoff from hitting really showed, and I struck out in more than half my plate appearances as an Expo. I did get five hits, though—even scored a run once.

HEY, BIG SEXY, WHO'S YOUR FAVORITE PLAYER OF ALL TIME?

Question

Jay Buhner,

when he was with the Seattle Mariners, as far as hitters go.

Nolan Ryan

is my favorite pitcher.

The Expos fell short of making the playoffs in 2002, and a few months later, they traded me to the Chicago White Sox. When I went to Chicago for the physical examination, White Sox management was very welcoming to me, and later, my new teammates and the fans would be just as welcoming. I really enjoyed my time in Chicago. In all honesty, I wanted to stay with the team, long term, after that season.

But in 2003, I was pitching for a new contract, and for the first time I was going to be a free agent. The White Sox offered me a deal to lock me up before the season began. But I turned it down because I was pretty sure I'd get a better contract if I were on the open market. Through my agent I did make a counteroffer; however, the team also said no. What remained most important to me—no matter the business side of things—was that I stayed healthy. If I did that, I figured I wouldn't have to worry about my contract much at all. That would take care of itself. Of course, staying healthy would also mean I could continue to pitch and help the team.

Thankfully, I felt great all year. I was able to make every start—thirty-four—and throw 242 innings, my career high. I thought I pitched pretty well, too, with a 3.87 ERA, and nine complete games, which was tied for the league lead.

After the season ended, I went home to the Dominican Republic and waited. The past couple of years in baseball there have been star players, like Bryce Harper, Manny Machado, and J. D. Martinez, who don't get their contracts done until spring training, or even later. I remember back in '03, there was a sense that the owners were trying to keep contracts particularly team-friendly—I'll put it that way. The market had been much kinder to the players in previous off-seasons. Many players like myself had to wait for what, back then, seemed like a long time to get a deal done. That day finally came for me in December.

I understand that fans want players to show loyalty to teams, and as a ballplayer, you love the fans; you do a lot of things for the fans. At the same time, fans have to understand that for us, baseball is a job—a very fun job, but still a job.

BARTOLO COLÓN

I was in El Copey, playing pool with my friends all day long into the nighttime. My agent at the time, Mitch Frankel, called five times with updated offers. As far as I knew there was only one team showing interest in signing me: the Anaheim Angels.

Going into the off-season I told Mitch, "I want $52 million for four years." I knew what other pitchers who'd performed similarly to me were earning at that time, and it didn't matter to me which team I went to. I'd go wherever they offered me $52 million for four years.

I understand that fans want players to show loyalty to teams, and as a ballplayer, you love the fans; you do a lot of things for the fans. At the same time, fans have to understand that for us, baseball is a job—a very fun job, but still a job—and when you're looking for something more and the team you're on doesn't want to give it to you, you're obliged to make some tough decisions. Like anyone else, when you have a job and are offered a better one elsewhere, what do you do?

The Angels started their bidding with $40 million for four years. "I said $52 million," I told Mitch, and hung up. Then they went up to $42 million. I told Mitch again, "$52 million," and hung up. By the third call, they'd gone up to $44 million. Then they went up to $48 million. Each time I just told Mitch, "It has to be $52 million."

There were pitchers much better than I was at that time who weren't getting big contracts, but I remained at that number. I don't know how Mitch felt about all this, but it was what I wanted, and he followed through.

On the fifth call from Mitch, a little after 10:00 p.m., he just said, "Bartolo, $51 million."

I said, "I'll call you back."

I hung up and then dialed my father.

I said, "Dad, they're giving me $51 million for four years. What do you think?" And he told me, "Son, you're the baseball player. You're the one who knows."

And so we went with that and signed.

The market for the players recovered a year later, by the way. I don't know if the owners all get together and decide when to hold out on offering contracts, or if they figure out when to offer less to the players than what would be expected, but it seems to me they might sometimes do that.

BARTOLO COLÓN

HEY, BILL STONEMAN, WHAT'S YOUR BEST BIG SEXY STORY?

Bartolo was number one on the list of free agents to sign. I had Kelvim Escobar as number two. I told Bartolo's agent that if I couldn't get a deal done with them, that I'd go to Kelvim. Initially, I didn't get the deal done with Bartolo, and so I went to Kelvim's agent and got one done with them fairly quickly. I thought we were going to stop there, but the Angels owner, Arte Moreno, had recently bought the team in 2003. He said, "If you still want to get another one, keep going after Bartolo, and offer him a little more money." And we ended up with two starting pitchers, and both of them had great arms.

Bartolo had the big year for us, with the Cy Young. We had some good teams. We'd done a good job of bringing up guys through our system—Tim Salmon, Darin Erstad, Troy Glaus, Francisco Rodríguez, the list goes on. But we brought in guys from the outside, like Bartolo, who made us very strong.

As general manager, I really stayed out of the clubhouse unless there was business to be done down there. So I didn't really get to know Bartolo that well as a person. He's always had a pretty big body but was one heck of an athlete. You wouldn't think he'd be as athletic as he was, and he probably could have played any sport he wanted with that athleticism. I'd seen him when he came up with Cleveland, and I was with the Expos organization. He just had that great arm, and he was a competitor. He had a lot to learn when he first came up, but he did learn. He'd started to turn a corner and command his pitches a bit better, and started to pick up on the value of changing speeds.

—BILL STONEMAN
Anaheim Angels general manager

12

I began building the Bartolo Colón Baseball Academy—which is dug into a mountainside close to where I grew up in El Copey—shortly after I signed that free-agent contract with the Anaheim Angels. At first, I wanted to build a stadium for the community, so we could have our own team in a Dominican League. Later, we began to see that there was a future in opening an academy.

There are hundreds of academies in the Dominican Republic, far more than in any other country in Latin America, from what I'm told. Building the academy was one of the best decisions I've ever made because I am giving the boys who live and play there an opportunity that I never got—an opportunity most people from where I grew up never got either. It makes me happy to give them that support, and soon I'm going to build a second academy, closer to where I played when I was a kid.

Around 6:00 a.m. at the academy, the boys who live there wake up and start swinging. They take their bats and hit a big truck tire standing up in front of them. An hour later, they're inside the stadium, fielding ground balls, having long-toss catches, and taking batting practice. If they're not swinging at balls, we'll throw them the caps from five-gallon water jugs. (If you can hit a blue plastic disc, a white baseball will be easy.) Me and my friends used to do that a lot when we were kids if we didn't have a baseball around.

Some days, the boys from the academy pack into a tour bus and travel for up to three hours to play teams from other academies, in places as far away as Santo Domingo. The bus has room for twenty, plus the driver, and has leather seats with my initials sewn into the backrests. There are a few rooster cages scattered around the academy grounds to make the place feel a little more like home. On the ground level of the building where the boys live, there's a full gym with free weights, weight machines, cardio machines, and a refrigerator with water bottles and a few different flavors of Powerade. There's also a kitchen and dining room next door, where a full-time cook prepares mountains of rice, beans, veggies, and roast pork and chicken for them to eat together. A few steps away from the kitchen is the recreation area. During their downtime, the boys and the instructors shoot pool, play dominoes, and watch TV.

The academy is solar-powered, which is more economical. There's a bronze statue of me in front of the stadium, too. It captures me in the middle of my windup. It isn't life-size, though; that would have been too expensive.

At any given time, around twenty to twenty-five players, aged twelve to seventeen or so, live there with free room and board. The academy is profitable, getting a percentage of the contracts the boys might sign one day. José Leclerc, a reliever for the Texas Rangers, got his start at my academy. A couple of other players have made the Majors, and some more have risen to the Triple-A and Double-A Minor League levels. Depending on their dedication, the boys sometimes stay for years at the academy, sometimes just a few weeks. Thanks to the great work the trainers and the academy's managers are doing, the quality of the training is getting better all the time.

There's a small museum dedicated to my life and my career at the academy as well. I didn't come up with the idea for it, but my wife, Rosanna, and I liked it, and we donated the space and some materials. There are team photos of me with the Indians, White Sox, Expos, and others; old uniforms of mine; and a lot of framed baseball cards. There's the nameplate from above my locker at the 2005 All-Star Game, a few baseballs that I drew designs on, and poster boards about the academy, my accomplishments in the Major League and the Dominican League, and my life in El Copey as a boy. There's the machine I used to remove coffee beans from their fruit casings and a cardboard cutout of my beloved Pancho, may he rest in peace.

I've bought up a lot of land and properties in El Copey and the surrounding area. If you look down the mountain next to my academy, there's a church that I built for the community. I recently bought a restaurant up the road, and I told the people who work there that firefighters, police officers, bus drivers, and other civil servants should not be charged for their meals. I also bought a fire truck for El Copey because the town didn't have one. After me and some firefighters picked it up, we drove around the area ringing the siren until we got to the firehouse. That was a lot of fun; people in town were so excited and happy, which made me happy, too.

I've built some houses for people who needed them in the area where I grew up, and every year, a day or two before Christmas Eve, I hand out about three hundred baskets of food to people in different areas, especially in the mountains, because it's very hard living in those places. I give out fruit, rice, beans, juice, wine, even rum so they can have it all for Christmas celebrations. I remember one time I gave a box of food to a man and it had an apple inside. He looked at it strangely, and I said, "Do you know what that is?" And he said, "No."

I've been giving out the baskets for twenty years or so, and, like with the academy, the fire truck, the church, and the new homes for people, it makes me feel good to be able to give back like that. I give thanks to God. For me, it's a blessing that I can do these things. When I was young, I always thought, "When I am able to help others, I will." I wish more people would think like that. I really do.

101

BARTOLO COLÓN

HEY, ROSANNA COLÓN, WHAT'S YOUR BEST BIG SEXY STORY?

He told me when we first met that he always had a desire to get ahead, to become a professional, to be able to help his family and people who were in need. He has a huge heart. He likes to help people very much. He works hard to achieve his goals. He does the best he can to be a good father, although it's been a bit difficult for him because of his job situation, but I always wanted to support him because I always could see he has such a big heart.

—ROSANNA COLÓN
Wife

After signing the contract with the Angels, I admit that I did feel some pressure to perform—though it had nothing to do with money, at least not directly. When you get a big contract like that as a pitcher, you're now the team's ace. That's where the pressure came from. The Angels were relying on me more than any team before.

In my first season with the Angels I had a 5.01 ERA, and there were many people in the media who gave me a lot of crap, saying maybe the contract was a mistake or that I wasn't worth the money. To that I say, first, I won eighteen games, which matters a lot in my mind. You pitch differently when your team scores a lot of runs for you, and I felt I threw much better than my ERA might have shown. I also stayed healthy and tossed over two hundred innings. Yes, at times it didn't go well, and I gave up more home runs than I would have liked: thirty-eight, the most in a season during my career. Sometimes you make mistakes as a pitcher and the hitters club it out of the park; sometimes they don't. Once you're an established pitcher, a good pitcher, tough times like that don't bother you much. You just keep relying on what got you to that point, and the results eventually turn around. I did want to do better, and I worked to get better that off-season, but overall I thought winning eighteen games and throwing over two hundred innings was a good year in the Major Leagues.

And then the very next season, in 2005, I won the Cy Young Award.

In late fall 2004, I arrived in the Dominican and rented an apartment in Santiago, away from my family, and went to work with a trainer, Angel Presinal, who goes by the nickname "Nao." I'd hired Nao while with the White Sox. I worked hard with him for about three months so I could be better prepared for 2005. That was when Nao introduced me to the elastic athletic bands that really work and fine-tune all your muscles, using natural resistance forces, not weight. I used the bands in my training through the end of my career. There's video of me on the internet working with them, doing jumping-jack-like motions, sometimes throwing my arms forward and stretching out the bands behind me. I don't even know how many of those I do in a workout. A lot. I also used to ride an exercise bike for many, many miles as well.

The extra training that off-season helped me a ton, and I came into spring training in good shape, which was the most important thing for me that year. By then I'd also gotten an excellent feel for the two-seam fastball. I first learned the pitch back in spring training of 1999. Before a game with the Atlanta Braves, I was working out in a gym with some of their players, including the Hall of Fame pitcher Greg Maddux, who showed me the two-seamer grip. I don't know if Greg remembers that, but I do. I wasn't really comfortable using the pitch in games until around 2002. But come 2005, with the two-seamer, I was a real four-pitch pitcher, and all my pitches were working that year, thank God. Having that many pitches means the hitters have to hesitate a little bit more before they swing, which can make all the difference.

On the wall in my clubhouse at the baseball academy, I have the scorecard from my twentieth win that year, along with a game ball, framed. It was a 2–1 victory against the Texas Rangers on September 20. I went seven innings and gave up only one unearned run. That was special.

Unbelievably, though, just as my best season came to a close, I began the worst, most upsetting stretch of my pitching career, and perhaps my life.

BARTOLO COLÓN

HEY, BIG SEXY, WHO'S YOUR FAVORITE PITCHING COACH?

Answer

Dan Warthen

of the New York Mets, though many pitching coaches
helped me a lot throughout my career.

In the first round of the 2005 playoffs, the Angels drew the Yankees. They knocked me around pretty well early in Game 1, and we lost the opener. But the team rallied back to force a Game 5 in Anaheim. I took the ball, got through the first inning, but couldn't finish the second. My back and my throwing arm were giving me some trouble going into the postseason, but in the second inning of Game 5, my right shoulder gave out on me. I felt a very hard, painful pinch there and came out of the game.

My fellow Dominican, Ervin Santana, pitched a great game in relief, and the Angels advanced to face my old team, the Chicago White Sox. But I couldn't pitch in the American League Championship Series; I was in too much pain. The White Sox beat us and then went on to win the World Series.

I was not in a good place mentally, to say the least. I was beyond frustrated because I wanted to keep helping the team, but from then on, I was never the same player, physically, either.

I'll never know exactly what happened to my shoulder at that time. All the MRI showed was that the whole area was very enflamed. I figured rest would give it a chance to heal, and I had the whole off-season to do that. Well, not the whole off-season, because in March 2006, I wore the jersey of my homeland, the Dominican Republic, in the first-ever World Baseball Classic.

I was so proud to represent my country in the tournament. Like, I think, a lot of Dominicans, I feel an obligation to show the world what our countrymen are capable of when given the chance. And I was definitely excited to be playing alongside what I thought was the world's best team at that time. We had Albert Pujols, José Reyes, Miguel Tejada, Alfonso Soriano, Adrián Beltré, Vladimir Guerrero, David Ortiz, and many other outstanding players. Once we made it through to the semifinals, outlasting the teams from Venezuela and Puerto Rico, we believed we would win the tournament, without a doubt. My arm did not feel 100 percent, but I pitched extremely well, giving up only one run in fourteen innings, six of which I threw in the semifinal elimination game against Cuba. I left that game leading 1–0, but we lost 3–1. After the game, we were shocked and very upset. We felt like we let the whole Dominican Republic down.

I mean no disrespect to the Cuban team, but they didn't have too many Major League players on their roster, not like the Dominican team. The result of that game shows you how crazy and challenging baseball can be sometimes. That day, the better team just didn't have it. Still, I give Cuba credit; they beat us and went on to the finals, though they were defeated by Japan.

After getting hurt in the playoffs, my spirits were raised for a little while, thanks to winning the Cy Young Award, the celebration down in Altamira, and the Dominican Republic's relative success at the World Baseball Classic. But over the course of my 2006 season with the Angels, my shoulder still bothered me badly, and my right elbow started giving me trouble, too. I think maybe I was compensating for the tenderness in my shoulder, and my elbow couldn't take the added pressure I was putting on it. Whether I'd pitched in the World Baseball Classic or not, my arm wasn't going to stay healthy that year. I ended up on the disabled list, and I thought my career was over. I kept trying to come back with the Angels in '07, which was the last year of my contract, but the shoulder issue just never went away. Strangely, I continued to throw hard—ninety-six, ninety-seven miles per hour—but I was in pain and did not pitch well.

BARTOLO COLÓN

HEY, ALBERT PUJOLS, WHAT'S YOUR BEST BIG SEXY STORY?

One of my best memories with him is when we were playing here, in Anaheim, against each other, he got me out, and as I ran back to the dugout, I pulled his shirt out of his pants. He was just laughing. He's got probably the biggest smile in the game.

I've known Bartolo for a long time, as a fellow countryman. He's a guy who worked hard, just really a loving person and a great teammate. He's a great guy, a great human being, who does a lot of things for his country, and he never takes anything for granted.

—ALBERT PUJOLS
Friend and World Baseball Classic
teammate for the Dominican Republic

In 2008, the Red Sox took a chance on me, signing me as a free agent. I was so happy to be on that team, especially because Manny Ramirez was there and so was David Ortiz, also known as "Big Papi." I'd faced Papi when he was with the Minnesota Twins, earlier in his career. But when I got to Boston, Papi really looked out for me. It was fun being around him and Manny, but the team's management and I didn't see eye to eye on how to handle my injuries. With Boston, not only was my shoulder still bothering me, but my elbow kept getting worse. I found out later that I had bone spurs.

The bone spurs weren't much of a factor on the mound, but they were causing tremendous discomfort between starts. I told management that my arm was bothering me and that I couldn't pitch, and they didn't believe me. When I did take the mound, I threw pretty well and my fastball was still at ninety-five. Management kept pointing that out to me, so I guess they thought I was lying and just didn't want to pitch.

So I left the team.

I was desperate and decided I'd undergo surgery for the first time. I had the famous Dr. James Andrews, who does many of those Tommy John surgeries, cut me open. That was September 2008. I paid for the surgery myself, and he took three bone fragments out of my elbow. One of them was about the size of the top of a pinky finger, which had been floating around my elbow on its own and would sometimes jam it up.

I was so proud to represent my country in the tournament. Like, I think, a lot of Dominicans, I feel an obligation to show the world what our countrymen are capable of when given the chance.

BARTOLO COLÓN

I rehabbed all winter, and in 2009 the White Sox brought me back, but the same issue with my shoulder kept coming up. My mind was crazy. I felt bad that I couldn't pitch well for the Angels those last two years, after they gave me that four-year contract, and I was upset that I wasn't able to play much for the Red Sox and White Sox. But these were acts of God, and nobody can always be perfect. And I appreciated the Red Sox and White Sox for signing me, too; I just couldn't stay on the mound.

Then, in late 2009, I was at a training facility in Pensacola, Florida, trying to get in shape for hopefully another big league season. I received word that my wife's brother, Fermín Vargas, the man who helped me ask my wife's father for her hand in marriage, had been murdered in the Dominican Republic.

On my wife's side of the family, Fermín, who everyone called "Ito," was the patriarch. Like my father on my side, whatever Ito told his side of the family to do, they followed his words. Everyone looked up to him.

I guess we'll never know why, but some men were hired to kill him. Four men with guns drove up to the front of his house and started shooting as he got out of his car. Two of the gunmen shot up into the air to keep people from looking at the scene from their apartment windows. The other two shot at Ito. Police recovered fifty-four bullet casings from the scene; there were bullet holes all across his car. Ito was hit six times as he tried to get into his house, and before the gunmen drove away, one of them yelled to another, "Make sure he's dead!" Then that gunman walked up to his body and shot him in the head once more, point-blank. Just after that, his wife, who was pregnant at the time, opened the front door and saw Ito lying in front of her.

There were some suspects who were either questioned or arrested, but as they say in the Dominican, "Money talks." Ito was a good man. He was a manager at a car wash; he didn't get involved with anybody bad. No one is in jail for his death, so it's all a bit of a mystery still to this day.

When I was told about his murder, I left Pensacola for the Dominican right away, leaving my clothes, my car, everything.

After Ito's funeral, I just locked myself in my apartment at the baseball academy for a few months, all alone, thinking about my life. I didn't want to come out of my room. I didn't want to do anything. I didn't play any baseball for a long time. Once in a while I'd go onto the academy field to see what the kids were up to, but that was about it. I'd also really ramped up my drinking, too, I'm embarrassed to say. I was in a real depression.

Throughout that time, the people closest to me would knock on my door and say, "Bartolo, you can still do it; you can still pitch. Go back to baseball, the game you love. It will help you heal."

Finally, in April 2010, I decided to have a second surgery, this one on my shoulder. It would be an experiment, and I was the crash test dummy.

BARTOLO COLÓN

HEY, MANNY RAMIREZ, WHAT'S YOUR BEST BIG SEXY STORY?

Every moment with Bartolo Colón is a story. He's an awesome guy. He's a guy who is always going to be there for you; he is someone you can trust, someone you can go up to and have a conversation with and he is there for you. That's all you need.

You never know a teammate, really, until you leave the team. When you're on the team, you spend a lot of time with everybody. But you really know who people are when you leave; you learn a lot about the people who keep that relationship going—not only while you were there but when you are gone. And Bartolo and I always talk; we always text each other. If I'm in the Dominican, we spend time together; if he's here in the States, we get together.

We have a really good relationship, and to hear that Bartolo called me his best friend in the game means a lot because we played a lot of years together, and I really got to know his family, his wife, and we had such a great time when we played together. He's a great guy. He's a guy who has provided for his family; he's worked hard to get to the point where he is. He's a humble guy, too; he never forgot where he came from. Bartolo proves that if you fight for what you want, you have a chance to be somebody in life.

It was an awesome experience playing with Bartolo because, like me, he went through some ups and downs, but by the end, he had a great career. Nobody thought he was going to pitch that long, but he did, and I'm proud of him. We come from the same country, and for us to get what we did is unbelievable. It was a blessing. He's also always considered the big picture. He's helped the people from where he grew up who needed it; that's what we're here for. If you can help someone who's on the floor, pick them up. It doesn't mean anything to keep all the money that God has given you, because when you die, you're really not going to take it with you, so do good things with that money.

—MANNY RAMIREZ
Cleveland Indians and
Boston Red Sox teammate

15

My wife's cousin knew a doctor who was looking for a patient—particularly a ballplayer, and an older one at that—to take part in a new type of stem cell surgery. I was up for it.

A group of Dominican doctors overseen by another surgeon from the US pulled out bone marrow tissue and fatty tissue from my hip, processed them in some way, took a very big needle, and injected the stem cells into my shoulder, where there apparently was a bunch of ligament damage. My rotator cuff was torn as well. They injected some of that stuff into my elbow, too.

Six months or so after the surgery I was feeling better—physically and, more important, mentally. I thank God for that gift of good fortune. So many people supported me; so many people pushed me to try to pitch again.

I tried out for the Dominican team that was getting ready to play in a baseball tournament in Puerto Rico called the Pre–World Championship. José Canó, the father of Robinson, the Major League second baseman, was the pitching coach of that team. He told management that I was the best pitcher in the tryout and that I should play with them. I pitched well in the tournament and then went back to the Dominican to pitch again for my beloved Águilas.

I continued to pitch well all winter long. Eventually, Tony Peña, the longtime Major League catcher and manager, who was still connected to the Yankees, told me, "Bartolo, I want to see you pitch because I'm talking with the Yankees to see if they'll take you over there." So I told him, "Tony, I will start a game with the Águilas. Watch me then," which he did. I also pitched for the Leones del Escogido, a team in Santo Domingo, and then in a winter ball league back in Puerto Rico. But before making just my third start there, Tony said he had spoken with the Yankees, who soon signed me and invited me to spring training, where I made the team.

By 2010, the Yankees had moved into a new stadium, which never felt quite the same as the old one. But it was such an honor to play alongside all those great players: Derek Jeter, Alex Rodriguez, Mark Teixeira, and others.

One of my favorite catchers of all time was there, too: Jorge Posada. He wasn't the everyday catcher by then, but I loved watching him play—I always had, though when I pitched against him, I also never wanted to face him. I remember one game in Anaheim against the Angels that year we were teammates: He entered the game behind the plate to replace our injured starter. As soon as the Angels had a runner on first, they figured they'd test Jorge, and the runner tried to steal second. But Jorge threw him out. That was a great moment, and we were elated for him. He showed them "he's still got it," so to speak.

The Yankees teammate I talked to the most, though, was Mariano Rivera. I was thirty-seven years old at that point, but he became like a mentor to me. He helped me stay focused on baseball, when I needed baseball most.

Mariano also got me to cut down my drinking, and I stopped drinking on flights altogether. I told him about how I was afraid of flying, and he said, "Look, if something bad happens on a plane, whether you're drinking or not drinking, we're all dead anyway."

He made a good point there.

He also said, "You sit next to me, and you drink what I drink."

BARTOLO COLÓN

HEY, BIG SEXY, WHO'S THE TOUGHEST HITTER YOU EVER HAD TO FACE?

Question

Answer

ALEX
RODRIGUEZ

If he ordered water, I drank water. And later, whenever I would ask for a glass of something else, he would always smell it to see if it was wine or alcohol. It was always either cranberry juice or Pepsi or Coke. I thank him very much for that. I don't think a lot of guys would have done that for me back then. I think we were drawn to each other because we were both veterans who kept to ourselves, so we figured we'd talk to each other. I do still drink on occasion, but nowhere close to as often or as heavily as I used to.

It felt great to be back in the Majors. At the beginning, I was somewhat uncomfortable with the Yankees because they had me coming out of the bullpen. But after they named me a starter, I gained my confidence again. That was what I wanted.

After my season with the Yankees, one or two teams offered me Minor League deals, which I was fine with. You still get an invite to spring training with a contract like that, and I was confident that if that happened, I'd make any Major League team. But the Oakland A's stepped up and offered me a Major League deal—in part, I was told, because the Yankees front office recommended they sign me, which was so generous of them. They told the A's general manager, Billy Beane, that I'd be a good influence on the younger players and a teacher to them as well. I can't thank the Yankees enough for doing that.

It was on to Oakland for me, where a lot of things really began to click, pitching-wise, after those lost seasons being injured. I was thirty-nine years old, and

Six months or so after the surgery I was feeling better— physically and, more important, mentally. I thank God for that gift of good fortune.

BARTOLO COLÓN

naturally, I wasn't throwing ninety-seven miles per hour anymore. I had to rely on my control and pitch movement, especially from my two-seam fastball, which I began throwing the majority of the time. I'd noticed that with decreased velocity, the pitch moved more than ever. It shot down and away from left-handed hitters and ran inside on righties.

With the two-seamer working, I could pitch to contact; it seemed all I needed to do was consistently throw strikes, and the hitters—who weren't going to swing and miss at too many balls—would get themselves out. With that approach I limited my walk count, which was crucial, and was able to throw a good amount of innings. It was a blessing from God: As I got older, I became a better pitcher.

But just as important as my new pitching philosophy was to my success was the fact that the A's front office and my teammates supported me. I think in part because I was a veteran, the players showed me a lot of respect and treated me well. I felt like I had no pressure on me. My personal problems—the mourning of Ito, mainly—didn't go away completely, but when I went into the dugout and onto the playing field, those thoughts were left behind me, back in my car in the parking lot, you could say. You can't bring your problems to work; otherwise you're never going to recuperate from things like that.

I was never worried about Major League Baseball investigating my surgery in the Dominican either. The league was looking into it because the doctor overseeing the surgery had used human growth hormone—which was illegal in MLB—in surgeries with other patients. Major League Baseball also thought we might have been up to no good because the doctor worked in the US, but the surgery was conducted in Santiago. I knew I didn't do anything wrong, and my attorneys felt the same way, so they also told me not to be concerned. There was no human growth hormone used in my surgery, and it was done in the Dominican because that's where I lived and because my wife's cousin knew one of the doctors who wanted to try the surgery. MLB closed the case after investigating for a few months.

HEY, BIG SEXY, WHO'S YOUR FAVORITE MANAGER?

Bob Melvin,

of the Oakland A's. All managers are different,
and mine were great in their own ways.

When I was with Oakland, I think that was the first time the media learned about how I drew designs on game balls after my wins. I picked that up from Omar Vizquel, the shortstop for the Indians when I was with the team. I saw him doing it once and asked him about it. He said the coloring was a de-stressor, something that took his mind off things.

Back then I would do a lot on the mound that frustrated me, especially walking hitters, which I did much more often compared to later in my career. I think a day after I pitched a game for the Indians, I was a little bored and started coloring a ball. It was very calming. I still have that ball at my home in the Dominican.

For years, off and on I colored a ball only from the games that I won, which became part of the superstition of the exercise. Every once in a while, I'd buy a twenty-four-pack of Magic Markers and, using the colors of the teams I'd beaten, fill in different designs around each of the game balls. I colored one ball for every win in 2003 with the White Sox and gave them all at the end of the season to the manager, Jerry Manuel. He was another special person in the game to me. He was very appreciative of the gift, and very surprised by it, too. When I was with Oakland, I started coloring the balls again after every single win and stuck with it from then on, giving most of them away as gifts.

One accomplishment of mine that I'm very proud of came when I was with Oakland: that game against the Angels, in Anaheim, in which I threw thirty-eight consecutive strikes, a Major League record. Like when a pitcher is throwing a no-hitter, during the strike streak my teammates in the dugout stopped talking to me and wouldn't sit next to me. I thought, "What is going on?" I had no idea.

In the half-inning after the streak was broken—on a pitch that was very, very close to being a strike, actually—one of my teammates, Jarrod Parker, who's another starter, said to me in English, "Did you know you threw thirty-eight strikes in a row?" I couldn't really comprehend what that meant, partly because he was speaking in English. I also didn't completely understand it because some of the balls I'd thrown were outside the strike zone. The hitters either swung and missed those pitches, or happened to put their bats on those balls, meaning they were also strikes. But then someone else in the dugout explained it to me in Spanish, and I was amazed.

I'm proud of that record because it shows the importance of throwing strikes in the Majors, which is how I was able to succeed in the later stages of my career. High velocity is helpful, but pitch control and movement and putting the ball over the plate are even more important.

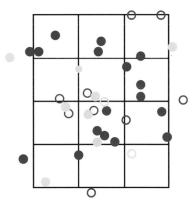

- ● Called strike
- ○ Foul
- ○ In play, no out
- ◐ In play, out(s)
- ◐ Swinging strike

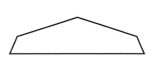

HEY, BIG SEXY, WHAT'S YOUR FAVORITE PARK TO PLAY IN AS A VISITOR?

Answer

Safeco Field,

home of the Seattle Mariners.

I do have to admit that my time with the A's wasn't all about fun on the field (throwing balls for strikes) and off the field (coloring them). Part of it was tainted. And it was all my fault.

In 2012, for a brief time I was using a banned substance. I tested positive for high levels of testosterone and was suspended for using performance-enhancing drugs. Major League Baseball caught me right away. It's the biggest regret of my career, easily, and when I was suspended, I was embarrassed for my team and for my family. Not only was I suspended, but I was also declared ineligible for the playoffs. And my father was so disappointed in me that when I called him and told him what I'd done, he was completely speechless. I learned later from my sisters, who were with him during the call, that after he hung up with me, he started weeping. My sisters were crying, too, as well as my mother, after my father told them the bad news.

The God's honest truth is that I never took any PEDs again. I know how much it hurt my career, and it was a huge mistake. I certainly wasn't going to put my team and family through another suspension, and Major League Baseball does a good job with its drug-testing program— when you get caught once, they test you all the time.

As my suspension neared its end, I was nervous about coming back to pitch because I didn't think the fans would treat me well. It turned out that I was correct. Mostly on the road, but sometimes even at home in Oakland, too, the fans would yell at me and call me a cheater. They'd even say it to me on the street sometimes, especially when I pitched badly. It made me very sad that I let the fans down like that, but I guess they had a right to be angry.

After the season was over, I wasn't sure that the A's would want me back. Why would they, after what I did? But by the time the World Series was over that year, Billy Beane gave me a new contract, which made me very happy. Before the suspension was announced, I'd approached Billy in the gym and apologized for my actions. All he said was, "Everybody makes mistakes; it's all right." Apparently he meant what he said. He's such a classy guy and showed me that again, in a different way, after the next season.

Though I was an All-Star in 2013, winning eighteen games, Billy didn't see a place for me with the A's in 2014, which happens sometimes, and I knew after such a good season some team would pick me up anyway. Billy called the New York Mets and told them they should sign me, that I was a good teammate and I'd help them out, especially with mentoring the young players. It was just like what the Yankees had done for me, and another example of how blessed I am.

The Mets signed me for two seasons and paid me $20 million. Even better: It was the start of one of the most fun and exciting periods of my career.

BARTOLO COLÓN

HEY, BOB MELVIN, WHAT'S YOUR BEST BIG SEXY STORY?

My best Bartolo story is also in a way my worst because it's when I had to tell him he wasn't pitching the deciding Game 5 of the Division Series against the Tigers in 2013. We had both him and Sonny Gray available to pitch, and it was Bartolo's normally scheduled day. But the Tigers were more familiar with Bartolo, and some of the hitters had really good numbers off him. Sonny had also pitched an unbelievable game against them earlier in the series.

Still, it was a really hard decision. Bartolo was in the Cy Young Award race for us 'til the end of the season; he was the guy who was there for us all year. I was up all night thinking about how I was going to approach it. The next day I had to tell Bartolo that

Sonny was going to pitch, and Bartolo made it easy on me. Like he always does, he just was a class act about it, said he understood, and certainly didn't pout.

In other games, when I would walk out to the mound deciding whether to take him out, I'd say to him, "How are you doing?" I got to know him well enough that, when he wanted to stay in the game, he'd just say back, "Good, how are you doing?" Everyone would start laughing out on the mound. He wasn't being pompous about wanting to stay in the game or anything, and it was kind of the same thing at the end of an inning. I'd go over to see how he was doing, and if he'd just look at me and smile as I was coming over, I knew he wanted to stay in, if he wouldn't look at me, I knew maybe he was about done; and if he had a towel over his face, I knew he wanted no part of coming out of the game. Those were the kinds of things that made it a lot of fun having him on the A's.

For years I'd seen him from the other team's dugout. I really didn't know what he was all about or who he was as a person. I just saw the guy who threw one hundred miles an hour and looked like he was always calm. But then I got to compete with him and have him on my team, and I got to realize he's worth so much more to a team, intangibly. He's such a great resource, showing young players how to go about their business, and with pitchers showing them the importance of throwing strikes, getting ahead in counts, fielding their position, being quick to the plate—all of those things that he'd developed over the years to make himself better. Then there was the subtle comedy that he was all about that was absolutely terrific. He's a great student of the game, but the personality more than anything is the thing that I'll remember. He was one of my favorite players that I've ever managed.

—BOB MELVIN
Oakland A's manager

I think most Mets fans will probably remember me for the good things I did on the diamond— or at least the moments when I was out there having a lot of fun. But my time with the Mets did get off to a rocky start, thanks in large part to my old team, the Anaheim Angels.

In the first inning of my third game for the Mets in 2014, I gave up three home runs in a row. Mike Trout hit one out to center; Albert Pujols sent one to left field; Raúl Ibañez took me deep to right. By the end of the game I'd given up four home runs and nine runs total. It was one of the worst starts of my career.

It didn't bother me one bit.

Those guys were good hitters, first of all, and I knew the bullpen was tired from the previous couple of games, so I stayed in the game as long as I could. I got through five innings, and over the course of a 162-game season, doing things like that are important. I still felt like I contributed something to the team, regardless of the score of the game.

Even though my ERA was 6.00 heading into my fourth start, the Mets faithful were about to embrace me as much as any fan base had before—though it mostly wouldn't be for my pitching.

I was starting for the Mets at home, Citi Field, against the Atlanta Braves. Their starter that night was my former Angels teammate, friend, and fellow Dominican, Ervin Santana. A day earlier I was talking to him out on the field, and I told him, "When it's your turn to hit tomorrow, I will throw you all fastballs, but you have to do the same for me." He said, "OK, no problem."

I still wasn't comfortable hitting at that point. It had been a long time since I'd been to the plate because I had been in the American League all those years, where they have the designated hitter in place of the pitcher in the

I still wasn't
comfortable hitting
at that point…
I wasn't even sure
where the best place
for me to stand in
the batter's box was.

147

BARTOLO COLÓN

lineup. I wasn't even sure where the best place for me to stand in the batter's box was.

When I went up to bat against Ervin, it was the second inning. The Mets were up 1–0, with two outs, and there was a runner on second base. It was my catcher, Travis d'Arnaud. I really wanted to get a hit and drive him in to help the team.

Ervin made it a little difficult for me.

As he promised, he started me off with a fastball. Knowing it was coming, I swung hard. But because I was so out of practice with the bat, and because Ervin threw the pitch outside, just off the plate, I missed. My helmet came halfway off my head, and I was so off-balance I almost fell over.

On the second pitch, he threw a slider. I swung as hard as I could again, but when I missed, this time the helmet came completely off my head, hopping around on the dirt in front of home plate. I was laughing on the field, not because of the helmet but because Ervin went back on his promise to throw me only fastballs. He sent my way another slider that went in the dirt, and I struck out. With each swing the crowd's reaction got louder, and I heard a lot of people laughing.

At first I was a little upset about that because I thought they were making fun of me for trying to get a hit and missing so bad. That was because of Ervin. But then I realized they just liked seeing the helmet twist around and jump off my head. After that game I told the Mets' equipment manager to give me a helmet that was a little bigger, so I could make the fans laugh some more.

BARTOLO COLÓN

HEY, DAN WARTHEN, WHAT'S YOUR BEST BIG SEXY STORY?

Every time he would start, before the game we'd play hide-and-seek. He'd come out of the locker room, and I'd be hiding. I'd have a tarp over me; I'd hide behind walls. I was in garbage cans, linen baskets. And he would always find me, and he would give off this belly laugh. Sometimes I'd jump out at him from inside a closet. It was like we were a couple of kids again.

That began probably about his fifth start with the Mets, in 2014, and continued on through his tenure there and into the time we spent together in the Texas Rangers organization. It didn't matter if we were at home or on the road: He came out of the locker room looking for me. It was part of his routine. He was superstitious about it, even.

That was the fun part of working with Bartolo. Also, in the National League, in spring training we have to practice sliding, even with the pitchers. When we'd start that drill, he would just raise his hand, wave his index finger back and forth, and say, "Bartolo no slide."

But what might be most intriguing is what would happen in spring training. It was like he would hold court. All the young Latin players would be around him, and I just remember walking through the locker room and there was like a tribe—a circle and he would be in the middle, just waxing, endlessly having great conversations, talking about baseball. He was like an icon or an idol. Even in Texas, players like Adrián Beltré, future Hall of Famers, would go to Bartolo's locker; he didn't go to theirs.

And he's the same person every day. He always walks in, says hello to everybody, knocks on the coach's door. Every day he is exactly the same individual—a big smile, is willing to help somebody. He's just a person you want to see every day, and you look forward to being seen with or being around because he brings energy to you.

—DAN WARTHEN
New York Mets pitching coach

It worked. There were many at bats where my helmet did some funny things—like when the earflap went over the front of my face.

But throughout that time I was getting more comfortable in the batter's box, and by the middle of 2014, I got my first hit as a Met, a shot all the way down the left-field line in St. Louis, which meant I had to run all the way to second base. I had to run some more after the next batter, Eric Young Jr., drove me in to score. I remember in the dugout the outfielder Bobby Abreu cooled me down, laughing, by fanning a towel. I needed it. And in my very next start I got another hit, too. Those were all the hits for me that season, though.

While I was with the Mets, sometimes I'd approach home plate and tell the opposing catcher, "Just so you know, I'm not going to swing at any pitches. Go ahead and strike me out."

The Mets needed me to pitch, not to hit, and on especially hot days at the ballpark, because of my weight, I didn't want to tire myself out at the plate—or, possibly, on the basepaths.

I would tell the Mets' manager, Terry Collins, "Look, I'm not going to swing without people on base." And he would tell me to do whatever I wanted.

If there were men on base, like that time against Ervin, I'd always try to take my hacks, though.

Once, against the Washington Nationals, Gio Gonzalez was pitching and Wilson Ramos was behind the plate. Nobody was on base, and I told Wilson, "I'm not going

152

to swing." He didn't believe me, and Gio threw me a curve-ball on the first pitch, outside the strike zone for a ball. I laughed and said to Wilson, "I'm serious. I'm taking all the way." The next three pitches were strikes, and I turned around and went back to the dugout.

153

BARTOLO COLÓN

HEY, TERRY COLLINS, WHAT'S YOUR BEST BIG SEXY STORY?

Early in 2014, our starting rotation was getting knocked around a little bit, so our bullpen was used up. We were in Anaheim to play the Angels, and Bartolo had a terrible first two innings of the game. He gave up five or six runs. He walked off the field, came into the dugout, came to me, and said, "Look, I know our bullpen's tired; don't worry, I'll get us to the seventh."

I'm gonna tell you something: You cannot teach that. He got through five innings, but what really matters was that he understood his team, what they were going through, and said, "I'll take the bullets." He wasn't worried about his numbers; he was only worried about the team.

The description of a professional? Bartolo exemplifies it. He came to spring training every year in shape. He's a great athlete; people never game him credit for being a good athlete. He had very quick feet, so that's why he could do all the pitchers' fielding exercises. He was such a good defender on the mound.

That play in Miami, when he threw the ball to first behind his back, is another moment that sticks out. At the end of the day, during spring training, Bartolo would actually practice that. And sure enough, it showed up in a game situation.

Bartolo just came to the ballpark and he did his job. You can't ask for anything more than that out of a guy who had been around as long as he had. He had to change the way he pitched after some years, and that's hard for some guys. But when he no longer had the ninety-eight-mile-per-hour fastball, he decided, "Hey, I'm gonna learn how to get the ball to move," and, cripes almighty, you talk about a guy who commanded his pitches. He had three pitches, but he used one of them all the time and just threw it to different parts of the plate, and commanded it. That just goes to show you, command is everything in the game. He was a guy who the younger pitchers, like Noah Syndergaard, could look at and say, "When I no longer can throw one hundred, can I still compete?" Bartolo could say, "Yeah, you can still compete. But here's what you gotta do; you gotta command everything."

And Bartolo was so looked up to by our Latin pitchers. I think the development of guys like Jeurys Familia and Hansel Robles was all attributed to the fact that Bartolo was on the team. He talked to them; he told them how to act, how to behave, how to be a pro. Those guys, in spring training, would go to a gym with Bartolo when the day was over and do exercises to keep their lower bodies strong, things we didn't do at the ballpark.

He could have pitched for me forever.

—TERRY COLLINS
New York Mets manager

Tragedy struck me and my family while I was with the Mets as well, though. My mother, Adriana, died from breast cancer on August 18, 2014. The night before, my wife told me to call my sister Miguela. I was so scared; I walked around my house, the top floor, the main floor, and the basement, trying to figure out where to call from. Miguela told me my mother was in intensive care and to come to the Dominican Republic because my mother was not doing well.

I also spoke to my younger sister Charo, who said, "If our mother dies, it is the doctors' fault." She was understandably very upset, but I told her everyone in my mother's life did the best they could do for her. I tried to get my mother to stay closer to me in the United States and receive treatment, but she didn't want to do that. She got treatment in her home, the Dominican Republic, where she was most comfortable. That was her choice.

Just three months earlier, my mother had been with me in my home in New Jersey, celebrating her birthday. Soon after that she was diagnosed, and on August 18, when I got off the plane in the Dominican, a friend of mine who worked at the airport, Miguelina, just said to me, "Bartolo, you have to be strong."

I knew what Miguelina meant. That was how I learned my mother passed.

It was excruciating, because we were so close and her illness so quickly took her life. It's still very difficult for me to talk about my mother. Her remains and a memorial are in a small cemetery on the road in El Copey where we had that parade. I visit her often and leave her flowers.

It was excruciating, because we were so close and her illness so quickly took her life. It's still very difficult for me to talk about my mother.

BARTOLO COLÓN

At the beginning of every season, most teams are hoping to make it to the World Series and win it. The 2015 Mets were no different, but I don't think many of us thought we actually would be as fortunate as we turned out to be. We weren't that kind of confident. During spring training, you look at the rosters of opposing teams and sometimes you think, "They're going to make it hard for us." In 2015, that was how we felt about the Washington Nationals. But we did use that perspective to motivate us against them and other strong teams that year.

We were in the race for the division at the end of July, when the league's trade deadline arrived. By then, our confidence had grown a bit. We heard the people on the radio and the TV saying good things about what we were capable of and how well we were playing, but it wasn't until the front office brought in Yoenis Céspedes that we really believed we could win the division and possibly go to the World Series. That move made us feel like we were being supported by management and motivated us to play well against *every* team.

Personally, I was happy to have Yoenis around, too. We'd played together in Oakland, but even before that I'd gotten close to him because he'd lived by me in the Dominican Republic, moving there from Cuba. So we'd get together, sometimes with our families, too. He's a tremendous person. Like my old friend Manny Ramirez, he has his own unique temperament, but he's a great competitor.

The night before the Mets traded for Yoenis, of course, was the game when Wilmer Flores, our infielder, was crying on the field. It was a sad, but ultimately beautiful evening. The fans thought they'd learned on social media that the Mets had traded Wilmer to the Milwaukee Brewers for outfielder Carlos Gómez. The fans gave Wilmer an extra round of applause one inning as he came into the dugout. I think one of them told him about the trade, too, and at first he thought it was a joke. But then we heard about the deal on the radio in the clubhouse. I saw Wilmer crying, and he said, "Why would they do

As I walked off the mound, I was sure to take a look at those wonderful Mets fans, cheering like crazy.

this? Why would they trade me?" Some of the coaches were talking to him, too. I hugged him and wished him good luck. I could see with his tears how badly he wanted to stay with our team. The rest of the players, who also got emotional, wanted him to stay, too.

Everybody knows now that the trade with Milwaukee wasn't official. Wilmer remained with us, and two nights later he hit that game-winning home run against the Nationals, pulling at his Mets jersey as he jumped on home plate. All of that brought the team closer and helped us stay focused down the stretch.

We did win the division, and I was thrilled to be back in the playoffs. But I was also a little nervous, I have to admit, because Terry Collins put me in the bullpen. I understood why he made that choice, but I'd never pitched in the playoffs coming out of the bullpen—I didn't even like the bullpen in the Minors, remember.

My first time with the Mets wound up being against the Dodgers, in Game 2 of the National League Division Series. There was one out, with runners on first and third base. I was worried about whether I'd warmed up enough in the bullpen. I just wasn't used to it, and you have to be very quick. Still, I got the ground ball I wanted and thought I had my double play to end the inning. But Chase Utley slid late and hard into our shortstop, Rubén Tejada, who couldn't make the throw to first. Ruben also broke his leg. The Dodgers scored the tying run on the play, and the umpires then allowed Utley to stay on second base. Eventually we lost the game.

BARTOLO COLÓN

HEY, BIG SEXY, WHAT'S YOUR FAVORITE HOME BALLPARK?

Citi Field,

home of the New York Mets.

I pitched in relief again in Game 3 and gave up a home run to Adrián González, but was fortunate enough to keep the Mets close to the Dodgers in Game 4, pitching two relief innings and giving up no runs. We lost that game to the great Clayton Kershaw, though.

Thanks mostly to Jacob deGrom and Daniel Murphy, who could not be stopped in those playoffs, we won Game 5 in Los Angeles to close out the Dodgers. Then we swept the Chicago Cubs in the National League Championship Series, and, incredibly, it was on to the World Series—my first and only.

When my mother died, a little more than a year earlier, my dad said he would never come back to the United States. I told my dad near the end of the 2015 season that if we went to the playoffs, I wanted to bring him to the US to see the games. And he told me, "The only way I'll go over there is if the team makes the World Series. If not, I'm not going." I said, "Well, at least come for the playoffs so you can watch me, and then you can go home." And he told me, "We'll see. First get in, and then I'll decide."

So we made it in, and my dad came to the US. From the beginning of the playoffs through the World Series, I had him with me, thank God. Once we'd gotten to the World Series, the Mets were confident we'd win it because we felt we had superior starting pitching to the Kansas City Royals, our opponent. I pitched well overall, even though, again, I was coming out of the bullpen. I got the loss in Game 1 but later came the biggest thrill for me that year. It was in Game 4 of the World Series, when

I struck out Salvador Pérez, the Royals' catcher, to hold on to a one-run lead. As I walked off the mound, I was sure to take a look at those wonderful Mets fans, cheering like crazy.

But the Mets came up short in the World Series, losing in five tough games. We made a few big mistakes and the Royals took advantage. After Game 5, the team was devastated, but the owner, Jeff Wilpon, came down to the clubhouse and said that they were going to bring the team back and try again in 2016, which we were happy to hear. I was especially excited because I was going to be a free agent again, so when he said that, I imagined it included me—and it did.

Even though a couple of other teams, including the Oakland A's, offered me more money, I stayed with the Mets the next year. It was the place that at that time felt most like a home for me.

Even if I had to hit.

HEY, KRISTIE ACKERT, WHAT'S YOUR BEST BIG SEXY STORY?

I like Bartolo a lot. He was a fun guy to have around, but we didn't start out the right way. He took one of those big foam rollers the players use to stretch their muscles out and, during his first spring training with the Mets, slammed it down on something behind me while I was talking to someone. It made a really loud noise and startled me. I wasn't happy about it, and I apparently gave him a look of death. He told a few of the other players that he was afraid of me or that I was not nice. That spring I just kind of scowled at Bartolo; he was wary of me. But at the end of spring training, we went to Montreal and as I was talking to someone, I get a tap on the shoulder and it's him. And he motions for me to follow him, and I do. He's standing there, and he says in English, "I'm sorry, I didn't mean to scare you."

After that he and I got along really well. He would do his best to speak to me in English, and he's pretty good. It's a little broken, but my Spanish is just as broken, and I'd try to speak to him in Spanish. So we would meet in the middle.

Shortly before his mom died, we were having one of those conversations in broken English, and it came out that she had breast cancer. He was just devastated; he kind of knew she wasn't going to make it. He was showing me pictures of her, and it was very sad. But after she died, he flew cross-country to make that start in Los Angeles against the Dodgers, and then flew back to the Dominican Republic for her funeral. In LA, you could see he was emotional and that he was on the edge of being very emotional the entire time. Still, he talked to the reporters after the game, and when that session wrapped, Ricky Bones—the bullpen coach who was doubling as a translator at the time—pulled me aside. He said, "Bartolo wants to talk to you another minute." I think he'd interacted with me a little more than the other reporters, so we talked alone together about his mom.

—KRISTIE ACKERT
New York *Daily News* Mets beat reporter

In spring training 2014, my first with the Mets or any other National League team, I didn't take any batting practice at all. I had a little bit of a sore Achilles' tendon that year. The two spring trainings after that, though, I did take batting practice. Between those extra practice sessions and all those regular-season at bats, going into 2016 I felt much more comfortable at the plate, and I wanted to do some damage against opposing pitchers.

I always had the goal of hitting a home run in the Major Leagues. Before I reported to spring training in 2014, I did take some swings on the field at my baseball academy in El Copey because I knew I'd be hitting with the Mets. I felt good at the plate, but considering the pitching ability at that level, and my extended time in the American League, it didn't take me long to realize how hard it would be for me to hit a home run.

But I did.

On May 7, 2016, I stepped into the batter's box at Petco Park in San Diego, a big field that had a long history of not allowing many home runs. I faced James Shields, an All-Star pitcher who was now on the Padres. It was the second inning. The Mets were up 2–0, with two outs, and there was a runner on second base. It was my catcher again, though this time it was Kevin Plawecki. I really wanted to drive him in and extend the lead.

By then I'd developed the practice of letting the pitcher throw the first pitch by me, so I could see his throwing motion and figure out how to time my swing. James started me off with a fastball off the plate for ball one. He threw another that was on the inside part of the plate, but for a strike. I thought, "If he throws another fastball, I'm going to at least swing at it."

And he did.

I swung hard, and it was like living in a dream at that moment.

I knew I'd hit a home run because the bat didn't vibrate. The contact was that solid. The ball flew a few

HEY, BIG SEXY, WHAT'S YOUR FAVORITE ON-FIELD MEMORY?

Answer

The Home Run.

rows back into the left-field seats, close to the foul pole, but it stayed fair.

I enjoyed my trip around the bases. As I approached first, the Padres' Wil Myers looked at me with his arms crossed, as if to say, "I can't believe you just hit a home run." After I rounded second, I said to the shortstop, Alexei Ramírez, a teammate of mine with the White Sox who I played a lot of dominoes with, "I can't believe I just hit a home run." I also remember seeing the 7 Line Army—that group of Mets fans that follows us across the country—going crazy. That was nice, too.

When I got to home plate, honestly, my knees were shaking, like after that game I pitched against the Yankees in '98 and the no-hitter in Buffalo. I was nervous but from joy.

Kevin Plawecki congratulated me; Curtis Granderson and David Wright, the next two Mets hitters, high-fived me on my way back to the dugout. Terry Collins, who was the only person in the dugout when I got there, gave me a fist bump. The rest of the team played that old joke on me—act like the home run doesn't matter by leaving the dugout—and it made me laugh. But by the time I made it to the end of the dugout they all came at me. I remember telling Hansel Robles, a Mets reliever, that my heart was accelerated because I was so excited. And all the starting pitchers—Steven Matz, Noah Syndergaard, Jacob deGrom, Matt Harvey—wanted to know how I felt hitting the home run, too. I just told them the same thing, that it was one of the most exciting moments of my career, that I couldn't believe it.

BIG SEXY

One of the best things about the home run is that many members of my family and friends were there to enjoy it, including my wife, Rosanna. I was eager for the game to finish so I could call my dad and tell him. After I was done pitching, I called him from the dugout during the last innings of the game. I swear, my dad was somehow more excited than I was, which also made me very happy. He said he expected it; he knew that one day I would hit a home run.

BARTOLO COLÓN

COLÓN LOOKING FOR HIS FIRST HIT OF THE YEAR HE DRIVES ONE! DEEP LEFT FIELD! BACK GOES UPTON! BACK NEAR THE WALL! IT'S OUTTA HEEERE! BARTOLO HAS DONE IT! THE IMPOSSIBLE HAS HAPPENED!

¡SACA BATAZO ELEVADO FUERTE PARA LA PARTE IZQUIERDA! ¡PA' ATRÁS,

BIEN ATRÁS!

¡LLEVA COLOR!

¡LLEVA SABO

OOOOOOOOO

OOOOOOOOO

OOOOOOOR!

¡HASTA LA VISTA, BABY!

¡CUADRANGULAR DE BARTOLO!

When the game was over, as I walked down one of the tunnels outside the clubhouse, the little boy who recovered the ball in the outfield stands—a Mets fan—handed it to me. I took a picture holding up the kid and the ball, as well as another ball I signed for him. His father only asked that I do that and sign a bat; that was it. And then, back in New York, the Guinness World Records gave me a framed certificate acknowledging that I'd become the oldest player to ever hit his first Major League home run, at 42 years and 349 days old. At the bottom of the certificate it reads, "OFFICIALLY AMAZING." I have the bat I used and the plaque in the basement man cave of my home in New Jersey. I'm not sure where the ball is, though. My wife put it somewhere.

When I was in spring training with the Rangers a couple of years later, I ran into the pitcher who gave up my home run, James Shields. By then he was with the White Sox.

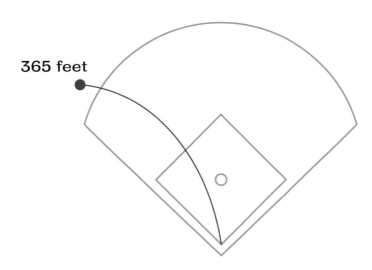

365 feet

He said something to me like, "Hey, do you remember that time you hit a home run off me?"

I replied, "No, I don't remember any of it."

I didn't want to make him feel bad. He laughed.

It was great pitching with the Mets, in New York City. It's more intense there than anyplace else. I loved it. I enjoyed the work I put in and am grateful for the support the team gave me, and the fans as well. In general, with any team, when you have the fans in your favor, even if you do something wrong, they applaud you. They also motivate you. You try to give more than 100 percent for them so they can feel proud of you and the team. And the Mets fans gave me their support, 100 percent.

I loved working with Dan Warthen, the Mets pitching coach. I continued listening to my coaches, taking their advice, like always, including Dan. I remember one time he said to me, "Bartolo, you're a Major League veteran— why are you listening to me?" I said, "Because you are my boss; I have to listen to you. That's just the type of person I am." We had a great bond. There was a lot of mutual respect; it was a beautiful thing.

I also worked closely with the bullpen coach, Ricky Bones. I speak English better than most people know, but I'm much more comfortable with Spanish. Ricky speaks Spanish, and sometimes I would watch the young starting pitchers—Jacob, Noah, Steven, and Matt—throw bullpens and give them tips through Ricky.

I'm not sure if the opportunity will ever come about because of the language barrier with me, but if I were

183

asked to be a pitching coach somewhere, I think I would like that. It would be an honor.

During my time with the Mets I also got my nickname: Big Sexy.

There isn't much of a story to that, though. Noah Syndergaard just started calling me Big Sexy in 2015, and the name stuck. I don't think I'm sexy, but if the fans like the name, I like it, too.

After I re-signed with the Mets for the 2016 season, on Christmas Eve Noah gave T-shirts to his family as gifts with my face on them, and they said "Big Sexy" underneath. He posted a picture on Instagram with his whole family—his parents, grandparents, everybody—wearing them. I thought it was hilarious, and so did everyone else. Noah gave me one of those shirts, too.

I'm not sure, but maybe a play I made on the field in Miami against the Marlins partly inspired the name Big Sexy. It was a game that I started on September 5, 2015. There were two outs and a runner on first base. Justin Bour was at the plate, and he hit a little grounder up the first-base line. I chased after it, and as soon as I left the pitcher's mound, I knew my best play was going to be to throw it behind my back. I figured if I missed, the runner at first base might get to third or even come around to score. But the Mets were up 7–0, so I could take that risk. I picked the ball up with my right hand and, with my momentum taking me into the Mets dugout on the other side of the first-base line, I tossed it behind my back to our first baseman, Eric Campbell. I got the out to end

I knew I'd hit a home run because the bat didn't vibrate. The contact was that solid.

BARTOLO COLÓN

HEY, DARREN MEENAN, WHAT'S YOUR BEST BIG SEXY STORY?

I loved having Bartolo on the team; he was such an easy guy to root for. I liked his demeanor on the mound. He could be out there, casually tossing the ball up and down after giving up some runs, where other pitchers in that spot might be stressing out. He always seemed very positive, so carefree. That's why a lot of Mets fans, I feel, were in his corner.

People come from all over the US and the world to cheer the Mets on with the 7 Line Army, at different stadiums across the country, wearing our T-shirts made just for the occasion. We were at the pregame party for the Mets versus Padres in 2016 at a bar in San Diego, and everyone knew Bartolo was on the mound that day. It was wall-to-wall Mets fans; one person had a Bartolo big head. I'm over near the bar, and these guys call me over and introduce me to this Mets fan who lives in San Diego. He's gotten tickets to the game and is going to sit with our group. They tell me, "This guy's gonna get a tattoo of Bartolo Colón if he ever hits a home run," and we all kind of laugh about it, like, "Yeah, that's never gonna happen."

Later on, we march over to the ballpark, and it's our biggest outing up to that point—we have more than 1,400 fans. We get to the game, we're in the stands, everyone's cheering, and Bartolo actually hits a home run. We go berserk. It was like we won the World Series, even though it didn't have any real impact on the season. It was just a home run, on a random Saturday in May in San Diego. But there happened to be a 7 Line Army outing there that day, and the guy hitting the home run happened to be Bartolo. It was the perfect storm.

Right after the home run, I think, *Where's that guy? He's got to get that tattoo!* I look a couple of sections over, and there he is—his friends surrounding him, pointing at him, laughing. But he manned up and got the tattoo done a couple of days later.

And the tattoo's huge. It's from his elbow to the top of his shoulder; it's got Bartolo's face with his helmet falling off, which would always happen when he took a big cut. It says the date of the home run, and it says "The 7 Line Army." It's not a great job, and I don't think anyone ever said that it had to be ten inches tall. He could've gotten something small and maybe gotten it covered later with something else if he didn't like it, but he can't get this covered. It's for life. I have an arm sleeve of Mets tattoos, myself, but that's a crazy thing to do. And for that home run to happen, an hour or so after the kid said what he did at the bar? That was crazy, too.

—DARREN MEENAN
Founder of The 7 Line

the inning, and walked a couple of more steps right into the dugout.

Pulling that off surprised me even more than the home run, because as a hitter I kind of have a say as to where the ball goes, if I get lucky with my swing. And a lot of people hit home runs in the Major Leagues. In that situation with Bour, as a pitcher, who knows where the ball will go? It wasn't anything I'd ever done before in a game in my life.

Many fans are amazed by that play, too, because of my weight. Sometimes in my career, I heard fans yelling at me things like "Fat boy" or "Eat some more hamburgers" or "Eat some salads so you can lose weight, you fucking fatty." They think I don't understand, but I do. It never bothered me, though. I used to say as a joke to my teammates who heard that stuff, "Listen to him, he's yelling at me, but he has to pay to get in here and do what he likes. I'm the one *getting paid* to be here, and do what I like, for a living." When it comes to my body, I feel good the way I am; that's all that matters.

One other special memory I have from my time with the Mets was when I pitched another game in Miami, late in the 2016 season. It was against the Marlins, and it was their first game after the tragic death of their pitcher José Fernández, who I was lucky enough to call my friend. We'd met at the 2013 All-Star Game, at Citi Field, when he was a rookie and I was still with the A's. He was a tremendous person, very likable and friendly, but he took pitching very, very seriously. We got to know each other pretty well.

We were supposed to go up against each other in that game in Miami, on September 26, 2016, and as the start time got closer, I thought, "Why does it have to be me to pitch this one?" I was not comfortable at all.

Before the game, the Marlins' Dee Gordon, a lefty who was batting leadoff and one of José's closest teammates, told me he was going to hit right-handed, like José did, for one pitch. He did, and I didn't want it to hurt his team, so I threw a ball. He switched to his usual left-handed batter's box, and I threw a two-seam fastball, straight but a little high, for ball two. Then, I followed that up with another one, right down the middle, and Dee knew what to do with it. He turned on it for a home run, and I was very happy for him and his team.

Dee was crying around the basepaths, and when he got into the dugout all the Marlins fans were standing and cheering. I held up the game, trying to get his attention to tell him to take a curtain call and acknowledge the fans. But he was so upset that, after all his teammates hugged him, he went right back into the clubhouse to be alone. I felt like crying myself.

189

BARTOLO COLÓN

HEY, RAY RAMIREZ, WHAT'S YOUR BEST BIG SEXY STORY?

There were some guys you could tell if they were pitching that day, or if they had a bad outing. Bartolo was the same guy, before pitching, after pitching—the same every day. He was unassuming. He didn't come in acting like a veteran who deserved preferential treatment over anybody else. Bartolo would come into the trainer's room on the days he pitched—and it's kind of an unwritten rule that when the starting pitcher comes in, everything else stops and the trainer takes care of him—and if he saw a rookie or anybody else on the table, he would say, "Finish with him, and then we'll do our work."

Bartolo had the shortest side sessions between starts of anyone I've ever seen in twenty-six years in the Major Leagues. He'd throw ten pitches—not even in the bullpen, on flat ground, and that was it. He'd say, "Hey, if I can't do it by now, I'm never going to do it. I've got to save my bullets for the game."

—RAY RAMIREZ
New York Mets head trainer

I struggled the last couple of years of my career; I know it. It was a challenge for me, essentially only throwing one pitch—the two-seam fastball—and with less velocity than I had before. Plus, you've always got younger players coming up who don't have that problem, and it makes sense that they get the chance to perform first.

But I still enjoyed my time with the Atlanta Braves and the Minnesota Twins. Both organizations gave me chances to pitch, which I appreciate very much.

I am especially grateful to the Texas Rangers for signing me for the 2018 season, after I had a hard time in 2017. The Rangers organization, my teammates, and the fans were all so good to me. They all seemed to really embrace my sense of humor, and we had a lot of fun times together.

With the Rangers, I was able to win my 246th game as a Major League pitcher, which meant that I had more wins than any other Latin American–born player in baseball history. That was the goal I had once I got my two hundredth win. I kept trying to come back and pitch so I could pass the Latino players with more wins than me. (At one point I also read an article by some writer who said I was too old to pitch and I wouldn't get to 246, so I also wanted to make him look bad.) I passed my Dominican brother Pedro Martínez, who had 219 wins; Luis Tiant, from Cuba, who had ten more than Pedro; Juan Marichal, another Dominican, who had 243; and finally Dennis Martínez, the Nicaraguan great who finished with 245 wins. (With each win, numbers 244, 245, and 246, Altamira had a big celebration.) The results on the mound, more often than not, were not what I was used to those last two years. Still, I wanted to beat out all those guys. And if I was winning, so was the team that signed me.

As an athlete, you always think to yourself, "I can do it. I can do it. I can do it." Even through 2019, I wanted to go back to the Major Leagues to help a team and to pass Juan Marichal again, this time for the record number of innings pitched by a Latino player.

That record is 3,507 innings.

After 2018, I was forty-six short, and no team signed me.

Whether or not I ever pitch in the Major Leagues again, I hope people who love baseball remember me for my longevity, how happy I was playing the game, how I treated people, and how I was able to build great relationships with them and the fans. To be honest, I would love it if the Baseball Writers' Association of America would elect me to the National Baseball Hall of Fame. I know that one big mistake I made with the A's hurts me a lot, and my career ERA, which is above 4.00, doesn't help either. The way the writers vote is out of my control; it's up to them. However, in my mind, and in the minds of my family, friends, and the people of the Dominican Republic, I am a Hall of Famer.

I don't live in El Copey anymore, but I visit once every few months. I still love El Copey and the rest of Altamira because it is always familiar, friendly, peaceful, and comfortable—it's still my home and always will be. I drive around the area and people see me through the windshield of my car and look surprised, but then they also smile and wave. I'll drive around the area with my friends on four-wheel, off-road ranger cars, too. (I had one of those for a brief time when I was a teenager, but my father took it away because he thought it was dangerous.) I go back to Rancho Nuevo and play softball sometimes, and many people I've known since I was a kid still call me friend and come up to me and chat, same as always.

I go to see my grandfather, who's in his nineties. He's blind and lost his leg a couple of years ago; doctors had to amputate it because of a disease. I don't like seeing him like that, but at the same time I give thanks to God because my grandfather is still alive. He still lives humbly, and happily, in a small house with a zinc roof—the same place he's lived since I was a boy. On the wall in the living room, there are a couple of pictures of me: one in my White Sox uniform and another of me and my father and friends holding my Cy Young Award plaque. My grandfather is very proud of me.

I always go and see my father as well. He's getting old, too, and has Parkinson's disease, so his arm shakes a little. But we can still talk for a long, long time whenever we are together. Today, he has a big farm with a bunch of people who work there. On the farm there are pigs and chickens and fields of trees that grow avocado, coffee beans, and cacao, of course. We play dominoes there and listen to music a lot.

I'm very happy about the way my career turned out; I'm very satisfied. But if I'm truly finished as a professional ballplayer, it's time to change my life. It's time for me to relax and enjoy myself and spend more time with my family and friends. Baseball requires so much dedication, and with the training, the games, the travel, it's difficult to be with the people you love the most. Of course, for me that includes my sons. I love them so much, and being a father is a beautiful experience. But I know having a Major League pitcher for a father has had its challenges for them. When you change teams, you have to live in the city where you play—and that might not be the city where your kids live. That's very difficult. While my boys were growing up, the most time we'd spend together was when they were on vacation from school. They'd come to wherever I was living and stay with me.

In May 2019, my wife, Rosanna, planned another huge party. It wasn't quite as big as the Cy Young parade, but it was nearly as special. This time we celebrated my forty-sixth birthday. The party was at our home in Vuelta Larga, just twenty-five minutes up the road from El Copey. We have about forty-five acres there, with a big swimming pool, outdoor dining areas, and a few residences. There's also a lagoon with fresh fish, a chicken coop, trees of avocado and cacao, and much more. Pretty much anything we could want we have on the farm.

My birthday party was held in the open-air nightclub on the grounds. We had a little over three hundred guests,

BARTOLO COLÓN

HEY, BIG SEXY, WHO'S YOUR FAVORITE PLAYER TO WATCH?

Question

Manny Ramirez,

when I played. Now it's

Freddie Freeman,

of the Atlanta Braves.

a big buffet, and a five-tiered cake decorated with the logos of all the teams I've pitched for, in the US and in the Dominican. It was topped by a baseball mitt. There were strobe lights and balloons; there was an MC, a DJ, circus performers, and a few live bands. There were many toasts to me, which was humbling and very nice, and everybody wore a different team jersey with COLÓN and the number 40 on the back. It was a beautiful gift that my wife gave me.

We partied until almost sunrise, and the dancing only stopped twice: when the dinner buffet opened up and when the party organizers ran a tribute video to me.

The video told my story, growing up in Altamira, how I picked cacao, coffee beans, and avocado with my dad, how I became a pitcher in the Major Leagues and won the most games by a Latino, how I built the baseball academy, all that. It had interviews with my father and a couple of my sisters, too. Toward the end of the video, a bunch of my former teammates and guys from around the Major Leagues—Hansel Robles, Noah Syndergaard, Robinson Canó, even Mike Trout—flashed across the screen to wish me a happy birthday.

My wife chose my forty-sixth birthday to throw that big party because it was the first year since I signed with a Major League Baseball team—when I was twenty years old—that we could celebrate the occasion with all my friends and family, at home, in the Dominican Republic.

Thank God I will have a lot more time for things like that, and the people I love to share them with.

I hope people who love baseball remember me for my longevity, how happy I was playing the game, how I treated people around the Major Leagues, and how I was able to build great relationships with them and the fans.

BARTOLO COLÓN

Epilogue

HEY, MIGUEL VALERIO COLÓN, WHAT'S YOUR BEST BIG SEXY STORY?

One morning, when Bartolo was about eleven years old, I said to him, "Let's go knock down some cacao." And he tells me, "Dad, I can't go. I'm tired. I'm not going today." I was very angry, but there was nothing I could do to get him to come. So I went out in the field by myself.

When I was there, I tried to take down a cacao, but it was holding firm on to the branch. I pulled on it hard, and when the cacao got loose, the branch came back and hit me in the eye—boom!

I was lying on the ground, and I said, "Shit, I almost took my eye out. So much work and so many lazy kids I have who won't help me."

I had a cut on my eye, and it was starting to swell. And suddenly I see Bartolo standing above me.

I said, "I thought you weren't going to come! You didn't want to help your father—now look at me."

He held up his right arm and said, "Don't worry, Dad. With this arm I'm going to make you rich and you won't have to work anymore."

And glory to God, that's what happened.

—MIGUEL VALERIO COLÓN
Father

Acknowledgments

206 BARTOLO COLÓN

Thank you to my family, friends, and everyone who has supported me throughout my career. I'm very appreciative to Adam Katz, Chris Sisto, Ceasar Batista, Angel Vargas, Meagan Ross, Garrett McGrath, and Michael Stahl for their hard work on my book. And finally thank you to all of my fans who have made my time playing baseball worthwhile and to God for all of the blessings in my life.

MICHAEL STAHL

First and foremost I'd like to thank Garrett McGrath and the entire team at Abrams Books for providing me the opportunity to write my very first book. It was an unforgettable experience. To Bartolo, as well as his representatives, friends, and family, words cannot express how much I appreciate the trust you put in me to tell this story. I thank you profoundly. I'd also like to extend gratitude to all of my friends, colleagues, and everyone else who provided me any morsel of support since I began my writing career. Much love to Lori for all her hard work and generosity, which, simply put, has changed my life in ways I could not have comprehended before we met. And, finally, to my family, particularly my parents, who told me to "do what you gotta do," thank you *so much* for your love and support.

MEAGAN ROSS

For Robert Francis Xavier Ross
Let's Go Mets!
I love you, Dad!
—Your Biggest Fan

About the Authors

BARTOLO COLÓN

is a Cy Young Award–winning and four-time All-Star baseball pitcher. He holds the record for the most career wins by a pitcher from Latin America and the Dominican Republic. He was the oldest active MLB player during the 2018 season

MICHAEL STAHL

is a writer from Queens, New York. His work has been published by *Rolling Stone*, *Vice*, *Vulture*, *CityLab*, *HuffPost*, the *Village Voice*, *Quartz*, *Mic*, *Narratively*, the *Brooklyn Eagle*, and elsewhere.

BARTOLO COLÓN

Editor: Garrett McGrath
Designer: Eli Mock
Production Manager: Kathleen Gaffney

Library of Congress Control Number: 2019939900

ISBN: 978-1-4197-4037-4
eISBN: 978-1-68335-800-8

Printed and bound in the United States
10 9 8 7 6 5 4 3 2 1

Abrams Image books are available at special discounts
when purchased in quantity for premiums and promotions
as well as fundraising or educational use. Special editions
can also be created to specification. For details, contact
specialsales@abramsbooks.com or the address below.

ABRAMS The Art of Books
195 Broadway, New York, NY 10007
abramsbooks.com